CULTIVATING A LIFE OF POWER

CULTIVATING A LIFE OF POWER

JASON RAWLINGS

Copyright © 2018 by Jason Rawlings

All rights reserved.

This book may not be copied or reprinted for commercial gain or profit. The use of short quotations or occasional page copying for personal or group study is permitted and encouraged. Permission will be granted upon request.

Contents

Acknowledgements	vii
Endorsements	ix
Foreword	xiii
Introduction	xv

The Journey

The Encounter	5
My Process	11

Identity

You are a Son	19
You are Loved	25
You are a saint saved by Grace	29
You are One with Christ	37
You are Fearless	43
Humility	47

Intimacy

God's Invitation	53
Importance of Worship	55
Importance of Surrender	61
Connect to the Source	67
Building your Secret Place	71
Tools to build the secret place	75
How to Initiate Encounter	81
Visions revealing the Kingdom	85
Your Heart is Key	89

Overcoming Offence	93

Walking a Life of Power

The Power of God must be seen	101
Power of the Holy Spirit	105
Accessing the Power of God through Love	107
Perseverance and Overcoming Disappointments	111
Fact vs Truth	117
Sympathy vs Compassion	119
Walking in the Prophetic	123
Operating in Healing and Miracles	131
The power of the Testimony	139
Practical tips to Ministering in Healing	141
Operating out of Rest	145
Your Turn	147
About the Author	149

Acknowledgements

I'd like to thank my wonderful wife for always believing in me and supporting and encouraging me to finish writing this book, without her it would not have been possible.

I'd also like to thank my Mum and Dad for their constant support and belief in me as well. My Mum spent many hours dedicated to editing and helping me with this book, it would not have been possible without all your hard work and support. A special thanks to my friends, family and the support from St Bart's over the many years.

I'd also like to thank all of the amazing mentors that I have had over the years. Indirectly, Kris Vallotton, Bill Johnson and all the other teachers at Bethel School of Supernatural Ministry. I wouldn't be the person I am today without your love and teaching and especially my direct mentors. Chris Gore, Les Coombs, Carol Campbell, Tony and Margie Scown and all the leaders at the Healing Rooms, thanks for being patient with me and always loving and supporting me. I greatly appreciate it.

Endorsements

Jason Rawlings' first book, Cultivating a Life of Power, is a very important book on the most important of topics. How to follow The Great Commission fearlessly in His Power. This is an easy-to-read book filled with basic tools and keys to walk in a Kingdom lifestyle where you know who you are, who He is and who you are together.

Jason is a man filled with a passion for seeing and experiencing the miraculous. You will learn, in a practical way, how to overcome life's hurdles by drawing closer to God, hearing His voice and operating in miracles, healing and the prophetic. This book is filled with wisdom and an intentionality to pursue the heart of God to be victorious in every circumstance in walking out your destiny. This book is a must read!

Carol Campbell

IAHR South Africa National Director

IAHR Africa Divisional Director

I can recommend this book to any believer who is desiring an intimate relationship with the Lord and to see His healing power flow through them.

Cultivating a Life of Power is a book that is very inspirational but also a manual on how to deepen your walk of intimacy with the Lord. It's a book about a young man's hunger and pursuit for the things of God.

Jason shares his journey in this book in such practical ways that birth a hunger within the reader to live a life surrendered to the Lord. It is written in such a way that covers many subjects from sonship, identity, hearing the voice of God, surrender and obedience, building the secret place, worship and warfare and spending time with a loving God who has invited us to partner with Him as His end time healers.

Jason is a seasoned minister of the word of God with such love and compassion, and is a wonderful mentor to those who would love to go on this journey of experiencing the Lord and His healing power flowing through them to heal the sick.

This book is a must read and it's an honour to endorse it.

Marie Bouris

Marie Bouris Ministries

Jason Rawlings from Roar and Soar Ministries can be described by the old saying "a wise head on young shoulders".

Jason has such a heart for the things that God has for humanity, within His Kingdom: relationship, healing, wholeness. He effectively unpacks deep truths with simplicity, in a way that is instantly usable.

Jason, along with his wife Melissa, have ministered at Intenciti Church on several occasions, teaching our congregation these very truths.

I love that Jason has written this book, because through this work, he will be able to passively disciple a multitude of people all over the world. As you read this book, you will be blessed.

Pastor Tony Scown

(Co-Senior Pastor Intenciti Church Brisbane Australia)

Foreword

We are living in a new day where God's focus is less upon the man of God, but rather the God of man. This next move of God is releasing the Kingdom through His body and empowering nations through the work of grace. For centuries the church has been displaying powerlessness, especially in the realm of signs and wonders. Certainly, the display of power can be uncomfortable and often misunderstood, yet its denial is not the answer. Rather, it is important we take the weirdness out of supernatural ministry and place the centrality of the cross back into the church. When Jesus is at its centre, miracles will flow.

Jesus is the exact representation of the Father (Hebrews 1:3). When we see Jesus, we see the Father. The nature of the Father is to display His goodness. Jesus modelled this: Jesus never welcomed a hurricane or an earthquake. Rather every storm He encountered was calmed and every person He prayed for was healed. Sadly, the church has justified their powerlessness to the level of experience, not truth. Hence, when it comes to signs and wonders, many have come to the conclusion it is not God's will to heal today. When the leper in Mark 1 approaches Jesus and asks, "If you are willing?" Jesus immediately clears up the confusion first before healing him. "I am willing," Jesus reinforces. The nature of the Father is to heal. After all, it is His name: Jehovah Rapha (The Lord who heals – Exodus 15:26). My pursuit over the past decade has been to recognise God's nature is His will and align my thinking with His.

Power is not our pursuit, Jesus is. A miracle is a signpost to a door. The door is Jesus. As we place Jesus in the centre of our own lives and look upon him we will discover new realms of faith, hope and love. Hebrews 12:2 reaffirms this, "Look unto Jesus, the author and perfecter of faith." If the body could turn their attention away from introspection and rather focus their attention upon the author and perfecter of faith, miracles would begin flowing in greater quantity and quality. Certainly as I have turned my attention to the heart of the Father and studied the life and ministry of Jesus, I have begun to see not only an increase in the quantity of miracles but an increase in the creative power of God. I am thrilled to be living in a day where Christ-centred believers are being empowered through grace for the impossible!

A key element to displaying increase is a greater awareness of your identity. Most believers sadly believe they are unworthy to be used by God. Our past sins and iniquities are used to disqualify us from releasing God's glory. Yet Ephesians 2 reinforces it is, "through grace we have been saved, not by works." Galatians 2:20 declares we were co-crucified in Christ and Christ now lives in us. The cross redeemed our misgivings and opened our life to the righteousness of God. When believers understand their worthiness is not merited by their performance but rather because of God's goodness, signs and wonders will flow. The good news is you are not a sinner saved by grace. You were a sinner but now you are a saint empowered through grace.

This is why I have no hesitation endorsing this book. Power must be cultivated before it is displayed. A garden that is not tended or prioritised cannot display the wonder of its potential. So too is it true in the Christian life. Cultivating a lifestyle of power is only possible through time in the presence of God, renewing your understanding of your identity and allowing the transforming power of grace to manifest through every part of your life.

I have personally watched Jason's journey into power, especially during his time at Bethel Church. Jason interned with me in 2013/14. I was greatly encouraged to watch this work develop within him. I was there for some of the miracles he describes in this book. Jason thoughtfully describes key themes to create a life of power and uses practical illustrations to stir your faith. Form without power is just another expression of religion. The church must display power to authentically display the love and grace of Jesus. I pray this book will position you to see such an awakening too.

Much grace,

Chris Gore

www.chrisgore.org
Director of Healing Ministries
Bethel Church, Redding CA
Author of Walking in the Supernatural Power of God and Overflow

Introduction

I was walking down a street in Mexico City with my friend Sarah. We had a lunch break and wanted to spend the time sharing the gospel on the streets, we had no interpreter but just trusted that God would lead us. We noticed an old man walking down the road limping, he looked like he was in a lot of pain so we went over and asked if we could pray for Him. At that moment a couple of the interpreters helping our team came around the corner. We waved them over and asked them to interpret for us to this man. We found out that he had a broken collar bone and a broken hip, however, he had no money to go to the hospital so he walked around in pain. He was also almost completely deaf in both ears and was 82 years old. We asked if we could pray for Him and then I laid my hand on his collar bone gently and began to pray. He acted very surprised and started speaking in Spanish to our translator, she turned to me and I asked what he had said.

She answered "He said that you pushed his collar bone back into place, when you laid your hand and prayed he felt his collar bone move back in to place and all the pain disappeared." I told her to tell Him that I didn't push his bone back into place but that it was Jesus Christ. She told the man who at 82 years old hadn't heard of Jesus. We then prayed for his hip and all the pain disappeared and he could walk on it. I laid my hands on his ears and prayed a quick prayer. I pulled my hands away and clicked and he started speaking again. The translator said "His ears are healed he can hear", we then shared the gospel with this man and, at 82 years old, outside the church building, he gave his life to Christ, and we led Him in a prayer to receive Jesus. He told us that he would begin to attend the church and left extremely happy and thankful for meeting Jesus.

Would you like to operate in the same supernatural power to see people come into relationship with Jesus? The good news is, *you can*! Anyone who has a relationship with Jesus Christ can walk in His power.

That is the purpose of this book, through sharing my life experiences, the obstacles I have overcome, the lessons I have learned, the encounters I have experienced and through studying the word of God. I will place keys in your hand to walk in the fullness of God's destiny for your life.

I pray that my testimony will release your breakthrough, that by the end of this book you will understand who you are in Christ, have a new passion to pursue intimacy with Him and understand how to cultivate a life of power. No matter your experience so far, whether you have seen the power of God operate powerfully through your life or you are yet to see it operate I believe that these keys will help you go to the next level and begin walking a life as Paul described. Not merely using wise and persuasive words but you will be walking and demonstrating the power of God to every person you meet and will begin to operate in the fullness of your destiny.

The Journey

My Journey

I grew up in an amazing Christian family, my parents were both in strong relationships with the Lord and raised us to place Him at the centre of our lives, to seek only Him. They were, and still are, attending an Anglican Church and this is where I was raised, amongst an incredible family of believers. I started attending church when I was one week old and I've never left, my Mum was my Sunday school teacher and I gave my life to Christ in her class when I was 9 years old. My Dad was the leader of a Boys' Club and I attended youth each Friday night. The Church was very close and embodied a family lifestyle, to this day I still consider the people there as my extended family. It had a very solid foundation in the word of God, and I was raised to know the word of God and I'm very thankful for that foundation, because it has served me so well over the years.

I would say that I have always known God, I can remember times in worship experiencing a tingling sensation through my body. I didn't know it then, but I now recognise that as being the presence of God.

I had my first encounter (that I can remember) with the power of God when I was around 15 at a church camp. They invited a guest speaker by the name of Stuart Gramenz to run the conference. Stuart ran "Jesus Heals" crusades all over India in the 80's and saw thousands come to Christ. I encountered the Holy Spirit on that weekend and I can remember crying a lot. I saw people falling over when he prayed for them, the first time I had ever seen that, and I was wondering why. Then a lady had one leg shorter than the other causing back pain, he asked me to hold her legs, which I did, and he commanded the leg to grow. I remember watching it start coming out and it went further than the other one, I was freaking out telling him it had gone too far. He waited and it went back to the same length as the other one and she was healed. I was amazed, I'd never seen anything like that before. I had heard of it happening but never seen it. For whatever reason I cannot remember seeing another miracle until I met that same man again 8 years later and my life changed forever.

Around that same time my friend (who was in foster care) found out who his father was and we started spending time with him. This did not end up being good for my walk with God, he did not know what he was doing and I have totally forgiven him now, but he was addicted to pornography, he swore a lot and was not saved. I'd never been around anyone like him before, and he showed us things that we should never have seen at that age. This sent me down a line that would take me several years to overcome, and added many challenges to my walk with God. I expect that will probably be a book of its own one day.

I continued going to church and was confirmed at the age of 16, this is an Anglican tradition, as a baby I was sprinkled with water and my parents promised to lead me into relationship with Christ. Confirmation is when I make the decision publicly to the whole church that I have made the decision for myself. By all outside appearances I was a good, godly, Christian boy who had a strong relationship with God and I would have considered myself in that manner. However, in hindsight I can see the truth and I know that I really didn't know God at all, I knew about Him but I wasn't living for Him or living in a personal relationship with Him. At this stage of my walk, apart from that one encounter with God's power on the camp, I had *no* power operating in my own life. I didn't know the Holy Spirit, I knew that we could pray for healing but I didn't know that anything would happen.

I was struggling in my relationship with God. The last couple of years of primary school I was bullied and that continued throughout high school, I was short and I believed in God therefore I was a target. This didn't help with my self-esteem and what I thought about myself. Even throughout this whole process I believed in God and served him, I had never touched alcohol apart from communion wine, I'd never seen drugs, or been interested in smoking or clubbing or doing any of that. God protected me and I honestly never had any temptation from any of those avenues. This didn't make me popular with the world who could never understand me.

This was the level of relationship that I had with God when I finished school and entered university. I had just turned 17 as I was born late in the year, and I headed to the Sunshine Coast to live and attend University. This was a totally new and foreign world to me. The first year, I lived in an apartment with 3 non-Christian guys, I soon found out the complex was called party central and I knew why. People weren't interested in studying, many of the students had come over from America, were 18 years old and just wanted to party and get drunk every day. There was a party every night and my room-mates would come back at all hours of the morning drunk and with the munchies, they would be doing drugs etc. Needless to say I saw a lot that year that I never even knew existed in the world. I was working on weekends and studying during the week, which meant I didn't have time to go to Church, and there were a couple of years there that I only got to attend now and then. I looked for a group up the Sunshine Coast and tried one connect group from Kings Church. The guys were really nice but the first time I went, they got in a circle and started praying in weird tongues and sounds and I couldn't understand anything they were saying. It totally freaked me out and I thought "what have I got myself into?" I just had no comprehension of the Holy Spirit at that time.

So, I spent those 3 years getting to Church when I could, and reading the Bible, and I would say I stayed in relationship with God, but I still didn't know Him and wasn't living for Him. Even so I did share the gospel with all my roommates over those 3 years and with people at university and school. I did the best I could with the revelation I had at the time, but I had no idea what I actually had available to me, and what I was about to walk into. I had no idea who I was created to be and who we are all called to be. During this time I was isolated and felt alone, and the devil played many mind tricks on me and dealt blows to my self-esteem. But God always looked out for me and protected me. He was always faithful.

I went back to Brisbane at the end of University and started working in Financial Planning. At this time my sister had started attending Garden City Church because there were some more young adults around our age so I decided I would give that a try. It was very different from what I had grown up in, which is not to say that one is right and one is wrong. I have respect for all Churches and all denominations, there are seasons of our lives and people feel more comfortable in different Churches and we need them all as the body of Christ. God took me on a journey through many different denominations, I believe He did this to expand my understanding and my love for each denomination, I now have a heart to minster to all denominations not just one. I grew up Anglican, my high school was Lutheran, then I attended Garden City Church which soon after I started turned into Hillsong. I started seeing people with their hands in the air, dancing around like crazy people. It was quite a sight to see and it helped me to start becoming more free in worship, although I had to force myself in the beginning; I would go up the front and jump around and dance with the rest of the youth just to feel free. I got connected with some great Godly friends and into a connect group with great leaders who role modelled Christ for me and helped me tremendously.

Around this time I had the encounter that would change the course of my life and start me on the path to pursue intimacy and personal relationship with Christ and begin cultivating a life of Power.

The Encounter

Up to this point, I believed that it was only special people who could heal the sick; you had to be anointed or be gifted especially for healing, or be a pastor because they were the only people I saw praying for them. I didn't see everyday people praying for the sick and seeing them healed, therefore, without every knowing it, I disqualified myself from ever being used. However everything changed in June 2008 when my parents invited me to an Order of Saint Luke Conference. The guest speaker was no other than Stuart Gramenz, the same man through whom I had experienced the power of God when I was 15, but this time was different because I had a powerful encounter with the word of God. The Holy Spirit revealed the scriptures to me, He transformed my mind and mindsets to be able to see the truth and I believe He is about to do the same to you as you read this book. Allow the Holy Spirit to breathe truth and dispel all lies that you currently believe. Stuart was talking about two passages of scripture I must have read a thousand times but never actually seen, but this time they came alive.

The first scripture is John 14:12 "Very truly I tell you, whoever believes in me will do the works I have been doing, and they will do even greater things than these, because I am going to the Father. 13 And I will do whatever you ask in my name, so that the Father may be glorified in the Son. 14 You may ask me for anything in my name, and I will do it."

The first point to note is that in the context of the scripture this is Jesus talking. He says, "*Whoever believes in me* will do the works I have been doing." The Church has placed a million rules around who can pray for the sick and when they are mature enough to pray for the sick, or if they are gifted, called or anointed enough to pray for the sick. How about we get back to using scripture and see what Jesus' qualifications are for praying for the sick. This is the one and only condition that Jesus used in His ministry, "*Whoever* believes in me." So I have one question, do you believe in Jesus? Yes! Then you are qualified to walk in the same ministry Jesus walked in, you can walk in the same power, miracles and healings that He saw each day. Note the scripture doesn't say the anointed man of God will heal the sick, or the pastor, or the person with the gift of healing, it says *whoever* believes.

But then He continues, "They will do even greater things than these." *Wow*,

Jesus himself said if we believe in Him we will do not just the same works but *greater* works than He did while He was on the earth. How can this possibly be true? Well firstly is Jesus a liar? No, so He won't give us a promise without giving us the power to live out the promise, correct? He gives us the answer in the next line. "Because I am going to the Father." Let's stop here for a second and look at this. What happened when Jesus went to the Father? Turn the page in your Bible and look at John 16:7 "But very truly I tell you, it is for your good that I am going away. Unless I go away, the Advocate will not come to you; but if I go, I will send him to you."

Who is Jesus talking about? When He left He sent us the Holy Spirit for many reasons, one being to carry on His ministry on the earth, the Holy Spirit is the very reason we can fulfil the promise Jesus gave us in John 14. Not convinced? Let's look at this a little more.

Just before this verse in John, Jesus is talking about the miracles that He has performed and He says that He cannot perform any of the miracles that He did but it was the spirit of the Father through Him who performed all of the miracles. All of the miracles that Jesus did He did as a man completely submitted to the Holy Spirit, He didn't do any of them as God. What does this mean? It means the Holy Spirit has performed every miracle that has every happened in human history including creating the earth. Every person who was healed, raised from the dead etc., through Jesus, Paul, Peter everyone, the Holy Spirit was the power behind the miracles. If Jesus did these miracles as God I would be impressed but I wouldn't be compelled to follow, however since He did these as a man I am compelled to follow, recognising He was giving me a perfect role model for life.

Romans 8:11 says "And if the Spirit of him who raised Jesus from the dead is living in you, he who raised Christ from the dead will also give life to your mortal bodies because of his Spirit who lives in you." This scripture shows that the exact same Holy Spirit who lived in Jesus when He was on the earth, and performed all of those miracles, was sent to dwell in us. You now have the same Holy Spirit living in you today to empower you to walk in the same power that Jesus did. Why? Jesus continues in John 14:13 "so that the Father may be glorified in the son." He sent the Holy Spirit so that you could walk as Jesus walked in the same power, doing the same miracles so that the world might know that Jesus lives today. He sent the Holy Spirit so that you might be living sign posts to point to the Father so that He may be glorified and men may be saved. He gives you a blank cheque to write on, "you may ask me for anything in my name and I will do it." *Wow.* Can you see how powerful you are now? Do you see the only qualification for being used is that you believe in Him?

It takes religion to make you think you are a loser. Kris Vallotton (Senior Pastor of Bethel Church Redding California) shares this illustration, if you are going to have a fight with your brother or sister and you can choose to be either a fish or a crocodile which would you choose to be? Religion would make you the fish, so you just lie there flapping around while the enemy kills you and takes you apart. However, God has created you as the crocodile, you are powerful, you are an overcomer and Satan is under your feet. You wouldn't see a child choose to be the fish because they know they are born to win.

When you believed in Jesus He qualified you, through the cross to be used by Him to heal the sick: He is worthy, He has paid for all of your sins, He has paid the price for all the sick to be healed. Jesus deserves to get what He paid for. Healing the sick is not about you it's about getting Jesus what He paid for. That should take the pressure off, He wants to heal the sick more than you do and it's not you healing the sick it's Him so it's through His merits not yours. By saying I'm not worthy or have done too many wrong things are we actually denying the power of what Jesus did on the cross?

So approach the throne of Grace boldly boasting in what Jesus did on the cross for you. Here's the other thing, if you think that you need to be absolutely perfect in everything you do and live a perfect life before God will use you, then you will never heal the sick because you are never going to consider yourself perfect on your own merits. Trust in the works of Christ and believe in what He has done for you. You are ready now to heal the sick and to be healed.

I'd like to share a story Kris Vallotton shared with us in first year at Bethel School of Supernatural Ministry in California, this story helped to change my perspective on myself and I hope it will impact you the same way. Imagine you are waiting in a room and there is a painting on the wall, you are sitting with a friend and he says "man that painting looks ugly, it's not worthy to be in a place like this it's disgusting." Do you think his comments are giving glory to the artist who created the painting? No, quite the opposite he is actually saying that the artist had no idea what he was doing and did a bad job. How do you think this would make the artist feel if he heard your comments? Not good. The painting is yourself, the model was Jesus because we are made in his image and the artist is God. If you spend each day condemning yourself, telling yourself how unworthy you are, how ugly you are, how imperfect you are, how do you think that makes God feel? It doesn't glorify Him it actually hurts Him. God does not make junk He makes priceless pieces of art. So next time you think of speaking badly about yourself, take a second and ask God how He sees you, how He created you.

No one knows who the author of this next little section is but I absolutely love it because it shows that God can and wants to use anyone.

Noah was a drunk; Abraham was too old; Isaac was a daydreamer; Jacob was a liar; Joseph was abused; Moses stuttered; Gideon was afraid; Samson had long hair and was a womanizer; Rahab was a prostitute; Jeremiah and Timothy were too young; David had an affair and was a murderer; Elijah was suicidal; Isaiah preached naked; Jonah ran from God; Naomi was a widow; Job went bankrupt; Peter denied Christ, The Disciples fell asleep while praying; Martha worried about everything; The Samaritan woman was divorced, more than once; Zacchaeus was too small; Paul was too religious and a murderer; Timothy had an ulcer; And Lazarus was dead!

What is your excuse as to why God can't use you? Do you really think that stands up now? God wants to use you, He paid a price to qualify you: all you need to do is believe in Him.

The revelation of John 14:12 and Romans 8:11 that day in June 2008 flooded my heart and mind and I knew that it was truth, I knew that I had been qualified by Jesus to be used to heal the sick, raise the dead and live an extra ordinary supernatural lifestyle destroying the works of the devil. In the last session of the conference he asked us to pray for anyone around us who needed healing. I said to God, if this is true then it will work. The lady next to me raised her arm because her other shoulder was frozen and she could barely move it. She was in pain and had no mobility. I believed that what God had said was true, so I laid my hand on her shoulder and I commanded her to be healed and her shoulder loosened. I asked her to test it out and see what was happening, she started moving her arm up and was about to tell me that she didn't know if anything was happening when something came on me and I grabbed her arm and started lifting it up. I can still see her face as I was raising her arm above her head and her shocked expression that her arm was going up without pain. I raised her arm up and down a couple of times and she began moving it herself, she said she felt fire going through her shoulder and all the pain was gone and she could move it. For me, that sealed in my heart that this was the truth and I would dedicate the rest of my life to pursing God and walking in the supernatural.

Perhaps many of you are in this place, you have had the revelation that the supernatural is for today and wondering, what should I do now? or How can I steward and grow this in my life? Keep reading and hopefully I'll be able to assist.

My Process

Once I had this revelation I started reading the word of God and pursuing Him. I began watching a Stuart Gramenz "Healing the Sick" teaching series with my best friend Greg Palma. We went through the series together and studied what the Bible had to say about healing and I started laying my hands on people and believing that they would be healed. I can't remember how it came about but somehow I was led to John G Lake ministries run by Curry Blake, and I watched his 19 hour series on "Divine Healing Technician Training". This further transformed my life as I must have watched 3 or 4 of these series a number of times. I was listening to the teaching 5-8 hours a day.

The very first time I listened to it, I can remember sitting in my bedroom and I was just crying the whole way through the series as I learned that much of what I believed had been lies and the Holy Spirit began to reveal the truth to me. At first the truth offended me, it offended my mind, but my spirit was leaping with joy celebrating that I was at last hearing the truth. I listened to my spirit and allowed the Spirit of God to transform my mindsets. I forgot everything I had ever learned and everything I had ever believed about healing and the supernatural and I started from scratch. I would urge you to allow the Holy Spirit to reveal the truth to you, agree with Him and let Him transform you. It felt like a painful process but at the same time highly liberating. Curry tore apart every evil doctrine that had been established by man and brought me back to solely the word of God and I'm very thankful for his teaching. I listened to it over and over allowing the word of God to wash over my mind and establish strongholds of the truth. I meditated on the word of God until it became real to me.

Then on the 2nd of October 2009 I had another encounter that would change me forever. I had been wondering about this speaking in tongues thing, why did we need it, was it Biblical etc. So I spent a night with friends studying every scripture we could find around the Holy Spirit, His purpose and speaking in tongues. We studied for hours and I gained enough understanding to know that it was Biblical, it was available and I wanted it. So the next day I went along to a youth conference at Hillsong Church, and was standing in worship with my hands in the air praising God and I just said "God I want it". Bam! I began crying as the presence of God overcame me and I began speaking in tongues, it was strange at first and I kept it a secret for a while. I went home and in the privacy of my own room I began activating this new gift that God had given me. You see just like any other gift of the Spirit speaking in tongues can operate through faith, it can sovereignly come upon you but most of the time it operates through faith. I would pray and invite the Holy Spirit to pray through me and then I would open my mouth in faith and begin to speak in tongues and God would fill it. Honestly, it was quite strange to begin with and took me quite a while to get used to, it wasn't until around 3 years later that I actually gained revelation as to the purpose of speaking in tongues and the power that is associated with it. When I gained that revelation you couldn't stop me praying in tongues.

I would highly recommend a book called "Walking in the Spirit, Walking in Power". It's the best book I've read to gain understanding in tongues, which I will talk a little more about later in the book, as it is an important key to cultivating a life of power. This encounter with the Holy Spirit changed my life again because it birthed in me a love for people. I began to see people as I walked down the street sick, dying and going to hell and began experiencing God's heart for them. It was overwhelming. At this stage I also began watching YouTube videos of Todd White doing street evangelism and seeing so many people healed on the streets. This was really a key to raising my faith to then go and do the same. I would encourage you to spend time watching testimonies of the past generals of the faith and the current ones. I would watch these videos and then begin to share their testimonies with people, I memorised every testimony of miracles that I could get my hands on and share them. As I did, it was increasing and building my faith to see the same miracles. I have spent literally hundreds of hours watching. Todd White, Pete Cabrerra Jnr, Thomas Fischer, T. B. Joshua, A. A. Allen, William Branham, Oral Roberts, Jack Coe, Kathryn Kulman just to name a few. If God can operate powerfully through those men and women He can do it through *you*!!!!

So I began to pray for people and people started being healed, not all of them, but at least some people were healed and that was encouragement enough for me to continue. Just to give you a very rough idea, I did not count the number of people I prayed for or the number who were healed, but I prayed for many people and maybe 10% were healed. If you focus on the 90% who didn't get healed you are going to end up getting pretty discouraged and disappointed very quickly. I learned early on that I needed to focus on the 10% and constantly give thanks to God that these ones were being touched, but at the same time I longed for so much more. It was a journey.

During this period of time I went through some serious ups and downs, what I would call mental breakdowns. The burden of the number of people who weren't being healed, when I knew that they should be because if they came to Jesus they would have been healed, that burden was immense I was carrying it squarely on my shoulders.

When you carry those burdens it doesn't take long before you breakdown and I spent many days crying, and crying out to God and having battles with Him. It was through this process that I learned that those burdens were not mine to carry and I needed to give them over to Him to carry. I almost gave up praying for people many times because the burden and pressure was too much, but God's Grace is always sufficient and His kindness is always towards you and He is always faithful. I will talk more about this in a following chapter on how to overcome these disappointments.

Let me be honest with you, as you seriously begin to pursue God, people around you are going to start considering you to be a little "weird or extreme" and not really understand and I experienced this *a lot* in those first couple of years. A lot of this misunderstanding will come through the people closest to you. The enemy will come and try and steal the revelation and the truth that God has placed in you. *Do not let him* do this to you.

When I first began pursuing the supernatural and beginning to understand my identity my family didn't really understand as many of my mindsets changed radically from what I was taught growing up and my parents still had these same mindsets. It was quite a battle in the beginning at meal times when I would share revelation and everyone would disagree and ask me questions. One time I came home and was sharing an amazing revelation about God's will to heal *all* the sick and my mother turned and said "who do you think you are?" I'm thankful for these times of testing because it just made my foundation deeper and stronger. It made me search the scriptures even more and seek God even more and made me so strong that I could never and will never be able to be moved from the truth that God *is* the Healer and that He wants to heal people all the time. I love my parents and my family with all my heart and I'm so proud to say that they are now my biggest supporters in ministry. They have been on the journey with me of changing mindsets and now I know that I have their complete support and they are proud of me. My parents have started seeing miracles through their own hands while they have been praying for people as well.

Never let people move you from the truth of the Gospel no matter who they are. One scenario when I had this realisation that people thought I was a little strange and didn't quite understand me, was at Hillsong Conference in 2010. I was becoming pretty excited and definitely stepping out more and at the conference I realised they had an entire section for the deaf. This grieved my heart, these people had come into the presence of God and instead of praying for their ears to be healed, we had catered for their illness. Now that was partly my immaturity coming out and partly the truth. So I talked to my friends and explained that I thought we should go over to the deaf section and pray for them all to be healed, to my surprise no one wanted to go with me. So, I went by myself. I walked over to the deaf section and caught the attention of the translator and asked if I could get permission to pray for each of the people, for their ears to open. The translator laughed to himself and said, "You can try but none of them will let you pray."

I was shocked, why would people not want to be healed? So he came with me and translated for me as I asked each person if they wanted me to pray for them. Not one of them asked me to pray for their ears, I did pray for a number of other things, mostly relatives or friends. This was highly discouraging for me at that time, but it didn't change the truth that God is the healer.

During the break we were waiting outside the main door when a guy came limping out on crutches with a massive leg brace on. My heart leaped with compassion and I ran over and asked to pray for him, he said that he had injured his knee playing rugby and couldn't walk on it and he was in pain. I prayed for his knee and asked him to put some weight on it: he tried and exclaimed that he didn't have any more pain. I asked if he felt comfortable taking off the leg brace and try walking on it, his mother was a woman of faith and told her son to do it. He took off the brace and started walking on his previously destroyed knee, no crutches and no pain. I prayed for him a couple more times and I wouldn't claim that his healing had 100% manifested when he left me, but he did walk away with no leg brace and not using his crutches, he was holding them under his arm. As you can imagine I was going insane with joy and praise to the Lord I just wanted to pray for anyone and everyone, those who were around me were excited as well. We must have prayed for every person on crutches that day another dozen people, one other person put down there crutches and nothing happened on the spot to the rest of them.

I'm sharing these experiences to encourage you not to give up when it seems that nothing is happening just keep praying, keep pressing in, your breakthrough is just on the other side of being uncomfortable, and who knows the next person may be the one who is healed. Ultimately your job is to love the person and it is God's job to heal them.

Another unusual event occurred at this conference on the day we arrived. I had driven the entire way from Brisbane to Sydney around 11 hours. We went to the city service where for the first time that I had seen one of the Pastors called me out of the crowd and prophesied over me. He said that I was a pillar to the church and that I would lead many into the kingdom. This is significant because as I was driving back from the conference to Brisbane I entered a series of visions and heard God say that He wanted me to quit my job and enter full time ministry. This was not on my radar at all. At that stage my plan was to be a millionaire by age 30 as I was going to work my way up in finance, make lots of money and then in 10 years or so enter ministry self-funded. Surprisingly this was not God's plan for my life and how glad I am that I have followed His plan and not my own.

I'm not sure if you can relate, but God is gracious and sometimes He tells me things many months in advance because He knows that I'm logical and I take my time to process things. It was a journey for me and took the next 12 months for God to change my mindsets and work on me to the point that I was ready to give up everything to follow Him.

One of the major mindsets that needed to be shifted was who the source of my provision was. One day the Lord said that I was trying to be my own provider rather than letting Him provide for me and that he wanted me to leave work and move into ministry now not in 10 years and He would provide everything. I also had too much of a focus on material possessions, a house, car, career etc. God began to move on my heart and completely change it. I now know that everything I have is His and He will provide everything I need and more. If I need a house He can just give me one.

During this period of time He set up a number of divine appointments which led me directly to Bethel Church in Redding California. Now honestly I did not know much about Bethel, I had read one book by Kevin Dedmon on treasure hunting, I had seen Jesus Culture perform and heard Bill Johnson speak once at a conference and at that time I didn't even know that there was a school. I just knew it was very clear that I was supposed to go to Bethel for 3 years to prepare me for ministry. During this time I also had the opportunity to pray for, and share the gospel with, a number of people in my workplace who were curious why I would give up everything to go study a supernatural course. In June 2011 I handed in my resignation, with 2 months notice, and in August I flew to Redding to start a brand new season of life. Nothing could prepare me for what I was about to experience over the next three years, life altering is an understatement. Really over the next 6 years, including that period at Bethel, I could summarise what I have learnt in two key words – Identity and Intimacy. Once established these will allow you to automatically operate in power.

Identity

I believe that Identity and Intimacy are the two *most important* areas of your life that you need to understand. Your natural response to finding your identity is confidence, boldness and power.

Personally, in my own life, God has taught me a lot about my identity through encounters with Him. These encounters are always taken back to scripture because God will never violate His word. The most common way for God to speak to me is through my imagination. He paints on the canvas of my imagination: I see visions and then He speaks to me the interpretation in my spirit which I process through my mind.

Identity comes through intimacy with Jesus and intimacy comes through identity, they are interlocked. If you understand your identity it will unlock the access that you have to your Father and this will increase intimacy with Him. At the same time as you become intimate with Him, He will reveal more about who you are in Him and who He is through you, and will teach you more about your identity which then leads you into deeper intimacy. I believe that these two areas are the most important areas in a believer's life. Intimacy and Identity mould vessels through which the Holy Spirit can flow.

Out of this place of identity and intimacy the supernatural flows effortlessly as does all the other fruit of the spirit and everything else in your life. If you are going to focus on anything in your life, focus on spending time with Jesus and finding out who He says you are. We will begin by exploring identity.

You are a Son

The first series of encounters that I had when I arrived at Bethel were all centred around one topic, Sonship. Let me clarify to begin with that when I say son I'm referring to both male and female as the bible doesn't distinguish, it refers to everyone as being sons. This was obviously what was most important for the Father to reveal to me initially before walking me through anything else. He began showing me the access that I had to Him as my Father and the relationship that I could walk in as his son using Jesus as the role model. This was the beginning of developing intimacy with Him. I went on a journey of moving from a slave mentality to becoming a son and understanding the access that I have to my Father. A slave does not know what the father is doing but a son does.

Galatians 4:4-7 "But when the set time had fully come, God sent his Son, born of a woman, born under the law, 5 to redeem those under the law, that we might receive adoption to sonship. 6 Because you are his sons, God sent the Spirit of his Son into our hearts, the Spirit who calls out, "Abba, Father." 7 So you are no longer a slave, but God's child; and since you are his child, God has made you also an heir."

Romans 8:14-17 "For those who are led by the Spirit of God are the children of God. 15 The Spirit you received does not make you slaves, so that you live in fear again; rather, the Spirit you received brought about your adoption to sonship. And by him we cry, "Abba, Father." 16 The Spirit himself testifies with our spirit that we are God's children. 17 Now if we are children, then we are heirs—heirs of God and co-heirs with Christ, if indeed we share in his sufferings in order that we may also share in his glory."

Galatians 3:26-29 "So in Christ Jesus you are all children of God through faith, 27 for all of you who were baptized into Christ have clothed yourselves with Christ. 28 There is neither Jew nor Gentile, neither slave nor free, nor is there male and female, for you are all one in Christ Jesus. 29 If you belong to Christ, then you are Abraham's seed, and heirs according to the promise."

1 John 3:1 "See what great love the Father has lavished on us, that we should be called children of God! And that is what we are!"

There is not much more to add really, these scriptures are so clear that once you believe in Jesus you become a son of God, Colossians 1:13 "For he has rescued us from the dominion of darkness and brought us into the kingdom of the Son he loves.". Once you were a child of the devil and now you are a child of God. The Holy Spirit is a sign that you are truly a son of God, Galatians says "Because you are His son He gave you the Holy Spirit and then the spirit testifies with your spirit that you are a child of God."

Take some time and ask the Holy Spirit to bear witness that you are a child of God. This is an incredibly simple yet amazingly powerful revelation.

The Lord showed me this transition in my life during worship one day. I had been spending time in my imagination going to heaven each day during worship and I saw myself in the throne room on my knees worshipping God, after about a week of this I had the following encounter.

I was back in the throne room on one knee worshipping God and the Holy Spirit said to me, "You are still in a servant mentality, you have been spending all your time worshipping me on the floor of the throne room which is good, there is a place to worship me as king, but you need to move into a relationship with me as your father and you as my son. Here are the keys to my house." and He chucked me a set of keys. "You are my son and have access to my mansion." Then the room changed and I saw thousands of angels in the throne room all throwing a massive party just dancing like crazy and Jesus was right there amongst us dancing joyfully, and He said, "Jason there is a time to worship and there is a time to have fun with me I enjoy having fun with you." Over the next couple of days Jesus began taking me through my mansion and I spent time in all the different rooms there, a room of joy, love, worship, peace and many others. Once I had the revelation of my sonship I began to search out what I had access to.

Now that we have established that you are indeed sons of God, it continues. This means you are heirs-heirs of God and co-heirs with Christ. *Wow*!!! Take a moment to consider what this means for your life. You are a co-heir with Jesus Christ!

This means you have an entitlement to the same inheritance that Jesus has, you have the same access to all of God's resources that Jesus has. You are a son with all the same rights, privileges and access to the Father that Jesus does.

Kevin Dedmon shared a story once about a servant and a son. Imagine that there is a house and they have a servant who comes in and does some cleaning around the house. You come downstairs at midnight for a snack and go to the fridge only to find this servant has let himself into your house and is eating all the food in your fridge. What is going to happen? You are going to tell him to leave and not come back because he does not have the right or the access to come into your house like that and eat from your fridge. Now the next night you come downstairs again and your son, who lives with you, is in the fridge taking some food, are you going to say anything to him? No, why? Because he is your son, he has the right, the access, to what is yours.

You are the son and you live in the house with the King of Kings as your father and you have access to everything that is His. The best thing is that, He says, "Ask whatever you want and believe that you receive it and it shall be yours." He is the richest Dad in the universe and He has given you a credit card with no limit and has all the bills being sent to His address to pay. He hasn't withheld anything from you, even His dearly beloved son.

As a child were you afraid to approach your earthly father and ask him a question? Were you afraid to ask him for something that you needed? Did you expect food to be on the table when you needed it, fuel in the car when you went places, a roof over your head? Did you walk up to your father and get on your knees and beg for mercy when you were sick or needed something?

I know that some of you would have, and I'm sorry for that, but most people would say "no." You had an absolute confidence that your father loved you and wanted to give you everything you needed. If your earthly father wanted to do this for you how much more do you think your perfect Heavenly Father wants to give you everything that you ask.

Do an exercise with me for a second. We usually place bad perspectives from our earthly fathers onto our Heavenly Father. Think for a second what a perfect loving father would look like, how would he act, how would he treat you? The Holy Spirit showed a picture of this to me once, the kind of access we have to a relationship with Him.

I felt the Holy Spirit show me a picture of heaven with God the Father sitting on the throne, Jesus next to Him and me sitting on the other side. Jesus right now is sitting next to the father 100% of the time in His presence and His peace, not worrying about anything, knowing He has instant access to anything He needs. He knows that He can just turn His head and ask His Father any question He likes and the Father will lovingly reply. The Holy Spirit said, "Jason you have access to the exact same relationship that Jesus has." As Jesus is *now*, so am I in *this* world! I saw myself sitting next to the Father in conversation. I hopped up and He stood up and lovingly embraced me as His son. This is the type of relationship to which you have access. God isn't a distant far off father, He is right next to you waiting eagerly for you to turn your attention to Him and begin spending time with Him, asking questions of Him.

Take some time to think about who your Father is and what He has in His possession. All of this is now available to you. His provision, healing, deliverance, freedom. More than this you are royalty, your father is the King of the universe, which makes you a prince. What does royalty have access to, how do they live? Your life will represent to the world who the Father is.

One of the reasons Christ was on earth was to show us an example of how we should live. Jesus was a man in submission to the Holy Spirit with the same temptations that we all face. He needed to know his identity and so do we. The most attacked area in a Christian's life is in the area of identity. The devil doesn't want you to know you are a son and he doesn't want you to know that you are loved. The first audible words that God spoke to Jesus were just before He began His ministry "this is my son, whom I love, with him I am well pleased" God established Jesus in His identity as a son completely loved and accepted by His Father. He is saying the same phrase over your lives today, "you are my son, whom I love, and I am well pleased in you."

Immediately after this declaration, Jesus goes to the desert and the devil says "*If* you are the Son of God turn this stone to bread." God had just told Jesus He was a Son and now the devil was saying if you are, prove it. Notice the devil left out a part of God's words here: God said "you are my son whom I love," the devil left out "if you are the beloved Son of God." Jesus replied (in my own paraphrased version), "I don't need to *do* something to know that I am the Son of God I know because God told me."

This needs to be your response as well when the enemy comes to you and asks you if you are a son. Just say, "Satan, I know I am a son because Jesus said I am a son, I don't need to prove anything to you so get lost."

For you to do this you need to first know that you are a son. Notice that it was Jesus knowing His identity that kept Him from bowing to temptation and falling into sin. The devil hasn't learnt any new tricks over the years, take a look at Adam and Eve – The devil came to Eve and said, "If you eat the fruit then you will be like God." In essence he was saying you can do something to become like God. However they were already made in the image of God. The devil lied to them. They were trying to get through performance, what they had already received through creation.

You are a son of God, a co-heir with Jesus Christ, you have access to the same relationship with the Father that Jesus has, and you have access to everything that the Father possesses. He is a perfect loving Father and if you realise the relationship you can have with Him, then you will begin to walk in the same confidence that Jesus had while He was on the earth. That is, your prayers will be answered, whatever you ask, because you can approach the throne of Grace boldly.

Changing your perspective of the Father

Most of the time, once you learn that you are a child of God and can have a relationship with your Heavenly Father, you then project your earthly father onto Him. This puts barriers between you and Him and makes it harder to relate to Him. This means that most of the time you need to repent, which simply means to change the way you think. You need to change your perspective of how you see God the Father. If you have had an absent father, or a father who was always busy and didn't have time to spend with you, or an abusive father or a father you couldn't trust or open up to, then you often project these attributes onto your heavenly father. What you need to understand is that God is a *perfect* Father and our earthly dads are not. Each of them have done their best in this life, but have fallen short of the perfection God has desired.

Begin to imagine what a perfect father would be like, how kind, generous, loving, compassionate He would be, what he would do for you, how he would speak to you. How would this make you feel? This is the Father with whom who you are in relationship, you never need to be afraid of spending time with your Father. He will never abuse you, He will never leave you, He always has time for you, there is not a second that you are alive that He isn't drastically in love with you. He doesn't have anything bad to say about you, anything condemning to say to you. He always encourages and builds you up. If He has some correction it is done in a loving way, at the right time for you to receive it. He knows everything about you, He knows you better than you know yourself. He knows the thoughts and desires of your heart. He knows your potential, He knows the hairs on your head and He only has good plans for you to make you prosper. He is *good*, He is always good and don't let any circumstance take you away from the goodness of God. As you take some time to think about what a perfect father would look like, take note of anything that is different between how you see the perfect father and how you view God at the moment and then take just a second and say, "Father I repent. I had an incorrect perspective of who you are, change my heart and my emotions to line up with who you really are, thankyou for showing me." Then live out of that revelation from this day forward. That's as simple as repentance is: allowing the Holy Spirit to reveal to you an area in which you aren't believing the truth, and then allowing Him to heal you and change you to line up with the truth.

You are Loved

For you to walk in absolute confidence you must have your foundation rooted and established in knowing how loved you are by the Father. 1 John 4:19 "We love because he first loved us." God is love. God's love is unconditional, you can't perform for His love. There is nothing that you can do to make God love you more, there is nothing you can do to make God love you less: He loves you 100% right now. Reading the Bible, praying, seeing people saved or healed will not make Him love you any more than He does right now. Many people are trying to seek God's acceptance and work for His love, but as you recognize how much He loves you, and how accepted you already are by Him, your natural response will be to love everyone around you. You will be working from the love of God as your source. This means all those things above will be a natural by-product of realising how much you are loved by the Father, you won't even need to try to do them.

Jesus' identity was established in the Father's love before His ministry began, the ministry came from love. God said at His baptism "this is my beloved son with whom I am well pleased." This is the foundation of Jesus' ministry knowing that He was completely loved by the Father.

Many of us are striving to be loved by God rather than recognising that He already loves us. It is actually receiving His love that empowers us to love Him in return. When I had this revelation I began to shift my focus from how much I loved God to how much God loves me. The more I realized His love and how much He has done for me, the more my heart would respond in love and I would want to do what He asked me to do. My response to His love, is love in return for Him and everyone around me. This love therefore, empowers me to automatically fulfil the entire law. Paul says the following in Romans 13:8-10 "Let no debt remain outstanding, except the continuing debt to love one another, for whoever loves others has fulfilled the law. The commandments, "You shall not commit adultery," "You shall not murder," "You shall not steal," "You shall not covet," and whatever other command there may be, are summed up in this one command: "Love your neighbour as yourself." Love does no harm to a neighbour. Therefore love is the fulfillment of the law."

While I was worshipping, falling more in love with Jesus every second, I got a fresh revelation of why I was created. I felt my Father saying, "This is why I created you so that I could love you and you could love me." It dawned on me that He actually created us for the purpose of having a relationship with us. He made us for love so that He could love us, we could genuinely love Him and we could love others.

This began the next part of my journey, where I began spending time asking God questions and experiencing His love. Here are a couple of things God shared with me personally. Who knows that when God asks you questions, He already knows the answers? You should really take note of questions He asks you because you will learn so much from them. He asked me, "what do you love about your closest friends?" My answer was, "it's not all the things they do for me, it's who they are."

God continued, "I don't love you Jason because of your works, I don't love you because you love me or worship me, I love you because of who I made you, who I created you to be, I love who you are. I love your worship, but that isn't why I love you. It's the heart behind the worship, the man behind the heart that is who I love."

God wants to have an intimate relationship with you: that is why He created you to walk with Him every day like Adam did. That's why He died to restore you back into this relationship with the Father. Abraham and Elijah were known as friends of God. Friends can only enter a certain level of intimacy. I want to be known as a "lover of God". What happens when you fall in love with someone? You can't get them off your mind, you are always meditating on what you like about them, you are constantly thinking about them. You want to spend all your time with them, you are willing to do anything for them. You will give your life for them. You will sacrifice to spend time with them. We should feel the same way about Jesus.

This week I want you to begin spending a short time with God and just begin asking Him some of the following questions, and wait to hear the responses from Him:

Jesus show me how much you love me?

Jesus why do you love me?

What do you love about me?

Father what do you like to do?

What are your nature, character and attributes?

Also ask yourself some of the following questions, with the help of the Holy Spirit, ask Him to show you the answers:

Jesus why do I love you?

What do I love about you?

What do I love about my friends?

What do I love about my wife/husband?

I found many of the times that the attributes you love about your spouse or friends are attributes that you are attracted to in God. We can learn so much from our earthly relationships about who He is.

You are a saint saved by Grace

I grew up believing, and maybe you did as well, that Jesus had died for me and He had forgiven me but I was still just a sinner saved by Grace and I still had a sinful nature. This meant that I was always going to struggle with sin my entire life, I would sin until the day I died because I will always be a sinner. Would you be hope-filled if I shared this as the Christian life and the accomplishment of Christ? Luckily there is so much more available for you to walk in as your inheritance.

One of the greatest revelations I had in my first year at Bethel School of Supernatural Ministry is that I'm no longer a sinner saved by Grace but a saint saved by Grace. I no longer have a sinful nature I now have a nature of righteousness, not because of anything I have done, but because of what Christ did. This revelation will help you to walk into more freedom in your life. If you believe and understand that you are a righteous son of God, with the same standing and relationship with the Father that Jesus has, would it not change the way you prayed? You would have the same confidence to heal the sick and raise the dead as Jesus did. When Jesus raised Lazarus from the dead He prayed, "Father I thank you that you hear my prayers and I thank you that you always hear my prayers. Lazarus come forth."

Knowing that you are the righteousness of Christ and your standing with God, will give you this same confidence when you pray. So I'm going to pull it apart and discuss some scriptures.

Romans 5:17 "For if, by the trespass of the one man, death reigned through that one man, how much more will those who receive God's abundant provision of grace and of the gift of righteousness reign in life through the one man, Jesus Christ."

You see you were not a sinner because you lived a sinful life, you were born with a sinful nature because Adam sinned. Just the same way you are not righteous because of the righteous acts that you do in your life, you now have a righteous nature because Jesus died for you and restored you back into right standing with the father.

1 Corinthians 15:22 "For as in Adam all die, so in Christ all will be made alive."

You see Adam died and all became sinners, Jesus died and all became righteous. I was spending time with the Lord one day and He decided to challenge my mindset. He asked me a question "Jason, why do you have so much more faith in Adam's sin to make you a sinner then you do in Jesus blood to transform you into His righteousness?"

When Adam was created did he have a sinful nature or a righteous nature? God said everything He made was good, we can assume then that Adam did not have a sinful nature when he was created. This means that when he chose to obey the devil and sin, his very nature was changed to a sinful nature and this was passed down all the way to us. I don't think you would have a problem believing when you got saved that you were a sinner, you had faith in the power of Adam's sin to transform your nature to sin. This is where most teaching has stopped. But here's the truth, when you received Christ into your life, you appropriated, by faith, everything that He accomplished on the cross to your life. You gained access to what His blood paid for. His perfect blood was shed on the cross not just to pay the price for your sin, but to completely wipe away any trace of sin in you; to restore you back into God's original creation. His blood was so powerful it transformed your nature BACK into a nature of righteousness. Now if you have faith to believe that Adam's sin transformed your nature to sin, then isn't it even easier to believe that the blood of Jesus transformed you back into righteousness?

The key to understanding this powerful revelation, is in the blood of Jesus. Did you know that when a baby is conceived none of the blood in the baby comes from the mother, all of the blood comes from the father? This is the reason that Joseph could not be the father of Jesus. The father of Jesus was not Joseph, it was God, therefore, where did Jesus get all of His blood from? Not a drop came from Mary, all of Jesus' blood came from God, that's why His blood carried the power that it did to cleanse the entire world from sin and transform your very nature from a sinner to righteousness.

Let's look at this further, 1 Corinthians 15:45 "So it is written: "The first man Adam became a living being"; the last Adam, a life-giving spirit." Jesus was the second Adam, He was the first man to be raised to new life. God sowed a son to reap many sons. When Jesus died and rose, He was the first son to rise to new life, but His death gave you access to become a son of God. Jesus showed you the life that God intended for you to live, one without sin. Jesus entered the world the same way that Adam did…righteous. Did Jesus have the ability to sin during His life on the earth? Yes, because He was a man tempted in all ways just as we are, however, He chose not to sin but to live in righteousness. Jesus and Adam both had a nature of righteousness one chose to sin the other chose righteousness. Sin is simply believing a lie and acting on it. I don't think Jesus was walking around trying not to sin. He knew that He was righteous before God and He spent time in relationship with Him, He knew God's voice and therefore He knew when it was the devil speaking to Him instead. Stopping sin in your life is not the aim of recognising your righteousness, it is the by product. As you spend time with God and learn to hear His voice more clearly, you also learn to discern the accuser's voice and not to agree with Him. You are transformed from glory to glory and the desire to sin simply isn't there anymore.

1 Corinthians 5:17-21 "Therefore, if anyone is in Christ, he is a new creation, the old has gone, the new has come! All this is from God, who reconciled us to himself through Christ and gave us the ministry of reconciliation; that God was reconciling the world to himself in Christ, not counting people's sins against them. And he has committed to us the message of reconciliation. Skip down to verse 21 "God made him who had no sin to be sin for us, so that in him we might become the righteousness of God."

You see through Jesus, God reconciled the world to Himself, which means He brought you and I back into right alignment or right standing with Him. Jesus became sin for you so that you could become as righteous as He is.

One of the things I was taught growing up is that we have both a sinful nature and a nature of righteousness which are fighting inside of us and we are dying daily to the sinful nature but it will be a fight to the last day we die and we just have to struggle to kill the old man. I don't believe this is true, you are not in a fight to kill the old man or to die daily to the sinful nature. Instead you are to simply receive the righteous nature that God has given you. Religion says you need to work for it. Relationship in the new covenant says you already have it and just need to receive it.

Colossians 2:11 "In him you were also circumcised with a circumcision not performed by human hands. **Your whole self, ruled by the flesh was put off when you were circumcised by Christ**, having been buried with him in baptism, in which you were also raised with him through your faith in the working of God, who raised him from the dead."

What happens during circumcision? The skin is cut away and it is now no longer there. Is circumcision a one off event or do you have to constantly circumcise yourself daily? Praise the lord it was done once and you never have to do it again. Paul uses past tense in this scripture saying it *has* already been done, your sin nature was taken away in a onetime event when Jesus died as you, you don't need to try and get rid of it any longer just realise that it is gone and receive the new nature of righteousness.

Romans 6:6-11" **For we know that our old self was crucified with him so that the body ruled by sin might be done away with, that we should no longer be slaves to sin because anyone who has died has been set free from sin.** Now if we died with Christ, we believe that we will also live with him. For we know that since Christ was raised from the dead, he cannot die again; death no longer has mastery over him. The death he died, he died to sin once for all; but the life he lives, he lives to God. In the same way count yourselves dead to sin but alive to God in Christ Jesus."

Galatians 5:24 "Those who belong to Christ Jesus **have** crucified the sinful nature with its passions and desires."

Romans 6 says two incredibly important things to take hold of, "we know that our old self was crucified with him" and "anyone who has died has been set free from sin." Paul says many times in different ways you are co-crucified with Christ. Paul identifies himself in Christ at his death, burial and resurrection, Paul says when Jesus died I died, this is how you can be set free from sin. The revelation has to come that Jesus died as you, you were one with Jesus when he died and you need to identify your death to sin on that cross with Jesus and you were raised a brand new creation with a nature of righteousness. You see Paul says if you identify yourself dead with Christ then that means you identify yourself raised in Him. Paul says "the death he died, he died to sin once for all". This statement is the same for you, at the cross this happened for you, you gain access to this reality when you believe in Jesus. "But the life he lives he lives to God" – the same is true for you. Then he goes on to say "In the same way count yourselves dead to sin but alive to Christ," what is he talking about? In the context of the verse Paul is talking about how Jesus died to sin once for all and now He lives for God. He is saying, identify yourself one with Jesus and count yourselves dead to sin just as Jesus is dead to sin. Does Jesus struggle each day with a sinful nature? No in the same way you don't need to because of what He did for us on the cross.

You can see righteousness foreshadowed all throughout the Old Testament through the sacrifices, but also through Abraham's life. Romans 4 talks about Abraham being credited righteousness by his faith and being circumcised as an outward sign and seal of him being credited righteous by Christ.

The Pharisees took this and made it into a work, creating the culture that circumcision actually makes you righteous. That wasn't the case, Abraham was righteous and therefore he was circumcised. It was a foreshadowing of the new covenant, Christ died as you and took away your sin nature and through faith you are raised in Christ and are not just credited but become the very righteousness of Christ. Righteousness is not something that can be earned or paid for it is something to be received.

Philippians 3:9 "and be found in him, not having a righteousness of my own that comes from the law, but that which is through faith in Christ-the righteousness that comes from God and is by faith." If you are still trying to fulfil the law and do enough right things or earn your right standing with God. Stop it, believe that Jesus has fulfilled the law and *has* made you righteous, and just receive.

Galatians 2:21 "for if righteousness could be gained through the law, Christ died for nothing!" If you could have been reconciled to God and made righteous by your own works then Jesus didn't need to die. Thank God for His sacrifice and receive the gift He paid such a high price for. This also means that you can never do anything bad enough to make you unrighteous because that would mean that sin has more power than the righteousness of Jesus Christ. Does this mean we should live an unholy life? No my point is, if your nature is now that of righteousness you have been empowered through God's grace to live a life of righteousness.

What does this mean for you? Sin is no longer separating you from God, you should now concern yourself only with meditating on the righteousness of Christ and learning what it looks like to walk out that righteousness. For the majority of people it is a journey of transformation rather than a one off moment. God showed me this as an example: I was once single, this meant I was rather self-centered because the world revolved around me and I could do what I wanted, when I wanted. In 2016 I got married and I was no longer single, I had been transformed into a married man. Did this mean that instantly all of the traits of my single life, all of my mindsets, my behaviours and actions instantly changed to represent that of a married man? Ask my wife, it took time for her to train me. If I made a mistake and left the dishes on the sink for two days, did it mean that I was no longer married and was now single again? No, it meant that I was a married man who had made a mistake. I had to renew my mind to the truth of being a married man and no longer single. It is a journey, and I have my wife and the Holy Spirit to help guide me and teach me what it looks like to be a married man. In the same way, when you give your life to Christ, you become a new creation, you become a son of God, you now have a new nature of righteousness. This does not mean that you won't make mistakes anymore, but if you lie to somebody it doesn't mean that you are no longer righteous. You are just being trained in righteousness by the Holy Spirit. Allow Him to teach you what it looks like, and agree to renew your mind to the truth of your new life of righteousness.

As you spend time with the Holy Spirit and allow Him to teach you about righteousness, you will naturally begin to walk more in line with this nature and the old will automatically pass away. You live out what you focus on. If you focus on trying to stop sinning, all you are thinking about is sin! So what will you do? Most likely sin. On the other hand if you become conscious of your righteousness, what will you do? Live righteously. You are what you meditate on. If you try to stop eating McDonalds, all you can think about is McDonalds and how much you want to eat it. However, if you shift your focus to that of achieving your goal of being fit and healthy and running around with your kids, then it becomes easier. Maintain your focus on your righteousness in Christ, knowing your identity and being established in who He has created you to be and what He has done for you.

So let's bring this back to how it affects us in the healing ministry. How you see yourself before God and the access that you believe you have to Him will determine how you pray and what you will believe to happen. Most Christians disqualify themselves and hide from the throne of Grace because of sin in their lives or many other things. If you understand what I've just shared with you, it will give you a new picture to the access that you have to your Heavenly Father, because of what Christ has done for you. You can stand boldly before the throne of Grace just as Holy and blameless before the Father as Jesus does.

He has qualified you in every way to do the same works as He did, to have the same relationship as He does and to walk in the same confidence that your prayers will be answered as Jesus did. When you stand before the presence of God He sees you just the same way as He sees Jesus; just as pure and righteous. If you understand this then you won't hide from Him if you sin, but you will run to His loving arms, you won't be afraid to come to Him with any request, and you will increase in boldness and confidence that He hears your prayers and will answer them. All guilt, shame and condemnation will be broken from your life through His empowering grace and love. The devil is trying to do anything he can to stop you from finding out this intimate, face to face relationship that you can have with your Father, He wants to know you so much, He paid a huge price for you to have this access and He wants you to use it.

How do you receive?

Romans 5:17 "receive the abundant provision of Grace and of the gift of righteousness."

Imagine I walk up to you and hold out my hand with a set of keys to a Ferrari that I have just purchased for you and say 'I love you so much I want to give this to you'. How much effort do you need to put in to receive this gift? What do you need to do? There is effort required, grace is opposed to earning but it is not opposed to making an effort.

God will never force something on you. He made you powerful and with free choice and He trusts you to make decisions. If I hold out my hand with the keys in it and you don't reach out and take the keys and say thank you then you won't receive the keys. They will stay in my hand.

God has paid the price and He is holding out His hand but we don't see it. We are still praying for things that He has already paid for and is actually trying to give us. We just need to recognise they are available and receive.

Once they receive, a lot of people then take the car and park it in the garage and continue to pray for God to do what He just given them the grace to do. If you don't actually use the car then you won't get anything done. The gift won't operate itself, God wants us to co-labor with Him.

Romans 5 talks about the gift of righteousness: a gift means someone else has paid the full price for it and there is nothing left for you to do but receive it with a thankful heart.

The more we understand the character, the nature and the goodness of the person giving the gift, the easier it is to receive from them. It is easier to receive from someone you are in a relationship with because you know the heart of the person and their motivation. Receiving becomes easier through relationship and intimacy.

We have this mindset that nothing comes for free, we have to earn everything, there's nothing without strings attached, and we transfer this onto our perception of God. This is not kingdom. Jesus paid the price.

We actually need to be more like children, they are great at receiving things that other people have paid the price for because they know that they are sons or daughters and they are loved. They have no problem asking you for something, asking is another way to position ourselves to receive. If I ask for something then I actually open my heart to the expectation that I will receive because I actually want to receive what I'm asking for. "Ask and it will be given to you." "If you lack wisdom ask and it will be given to you." You aren't going to reject something that you asked for. So begin to ask your Heavenly Father for things, but don't just stop there, when you ask expect to receive and begin to thank Him for giving you the desires of your heart. Thank Him for the gift of righteousness, thank Him for forgiving you. What you give thanks for increases; thanksgiving is a huge key in the kingdom.

You are One with Christ

1 Corinthians 6:17 "But he who is joined to the Lord becomes one spirit with him." Our unity and oneness with Christ is a very powerful revelation in which to walk. When you understand this, it will change the way you pray and the way you approach various situations, especially with the demonic.

During times of worship, God has revealed many times to me, in different ways, my oneness with Him. I will share a couple of different ways that He has explained this oneness, in the hope that it will speak to each of you differently, and help you to understand. I think one of the closest earthly illustrations is marriage. When we get married we make a covenant with each other, and the Bible says that we become one. However, after your wedding day two separate people still exist, you now begin the journey of becoming one. Joining together to create one unified team. Likewise with God, it doesn't mean that you cease to exist or now God uses you like a puppet making you do whatever He wants. You still have to live on this earth, however, you learn to live a surrendered life, laying your will at the feet of Jesus and allowing His will to take place through your life.

When you are married, you get access to your spouse's heart in a way that you never did before. You get to know their goals and their desires, and over time, your goals and desires will merge so that your goals and desires become the same. I know that now I have the ability to know the heart of my wife much more deeply, and to know the secrets of her heart and the depths of her heart. It is the same way with God. You get to spend time with Him, to know His heart and become unified in your desires and your will, so that you desire and want what God wants. You get to a place where it's not His desire and goals that you are working towards but it is your desire and goal to achieve His purpose for your life. You come into alignment with His heart. This takes time and effort, you have to make choices because you will always have free will and therefore you have to choose to stay in alignment with God.

This free will makes the transformation of your mind so important. Romans 12:2 "Do not conform to the pattern of this world, but be transformed by the renewing of your mind." What are you renewing your mind into alignment with? Your identity as a loved, righteous son, a brand new creation. 2 Corinthians 5:17 "If anyone is in Christ, the new creation has come: The old has gone, the new is here!" You are now a brand new creation. You have a new identity, a new name; you are a son of God. Your body is infused with His presence as the Holy Spirit comes and makes His dwelling in you. You now have the mind of Christ, and you should have the same thoughts in your head that Christ has in His. This will happen as you renew your mind through reading the word of God, but anything in your mind that wouldn't be in His, should be cast out. You have access to His divine insight and thoughts, but not just that, you have access to know His heart.

Another part of marriage is the covenant. In a covenant two parties come together and they make promises. You promise all of yourself to your spouse: your weaknesses, your strengths, your failures, your successes, all your wealth and possessions, all of your debts, all of your alliances and connections and all of your enemies. In the same way you receive all of these things as well. Here's an amazing truth: when you accept Christ, through His blood and relationship with Him, you become one with Him and gain access to the covenant that *Jesus has made with the Father*. You get all of the benefits: you get access to all of God's strengths, His wealth and abundance, His provision and connections, His love, healing, deliverance, power. You now have access to everything that belongs to Him but He also now has access to everything that makes up your life. That is how the weak can say they are strong. His strength is perfected in your weakness. You are now able to do and accomplish many things that you were never able to accomplish on your own. Do you see the power of being in covenant with God? Let's say your husband or wife is $100k in debt when you marry, however, you have a million dollars in the bank. When you get married, you pay off the debt and your husband or wife no longer has debt, but abundance. In every way your life is increased through covenant with God. As you realise your identity, what you have access to, then you can take hold of all that God has and apply it to your life through faith.

I'd like to take a second to look more closely at what it means to be in union with Him because I know many people will struggle with how you can actually be one with God. To understand this you need to take a look at the trinity, your relationship with the trinity and what happened at the cross. The Trinity is the Father, Son and Holy Spirit, each are individually separate but at the exact same time all are one and all are God.

Jesus is your role model. Jesus became totally human, Philippians 2:8, John 1:14, however, He was still totally God, He was human, however in the spirit, He was still one with God, because the trinity is one. Jesus is the key to why you can have this union with God. Jesus became human and died on the cross, however when He was raised from the dead and ascended into heaven, He was still human. Therefore He grafted all of mankind into the trinity, for whoever believes. It says in Romans 6 that "we are dead to sin but alive in Christ," Ephesians 2:6 says "we are seated in heavenly places in Christ Jesus". Galatians 2:20 says "I have been crucified with Christ and I no longer live, but Christ lives in me." Jesus didn't just die for you, He died as you, and when you identify yourself dead with Christ and raised in Him, you begin to understand that through Jesus you are now one with God. You are grafted into the trinity in Jesus, the trinity doesn't change however you get access because you are now in Jesus.

This then raises the question how did Jesus relate to the Father and Holy Spirit in his life. Jesus spent a lot of time in the secret place with the Father and he gives us this powerful secret into ministry in John 5:19 "Jesus gave them this answer: "Very truly I tell you, the Son can do nothing by himself; he can do only what he sees his Father doing, because whatever the Father does the Son also does." I believe that Jesus had his identity established by the Father and was given directions or revelation by the Father and then as he released the words the Father had given him or did the actions he saw the Father doing the Holy Spirit was released through him as the power to perform what was said. Jesus did make mention once in Luke 5:17 "the power of the Lord was with Jesus to heal the sick." I believe this was talking about the Holy Spirit operating with Jesus. We need to have this same relationship with the trinity, we worship Jesus for the sacrifice that He made and the access that He has given to us through His life. Everything we walk in, everything we get to receive in life is because of Jesus. We need to daily spend a lot of time in the secret place with the Father, finding out His goodness and allowing Him to establish our identity; finding out His plans for the day, seeing what He is saying and doing that day. Then we need to release what we see Him do and say and trust that the power of the Holy Spirit will accomplish the word of the Lord. Psalm 103 "As will the angels harken to the voice of the Lord and carry out his word."

Now that you have become one with Him you are now empowered with the strength, power and authority to overcome anything in your life. There is no devil too big or too strong that you cannot take out. Once I realised this, I saw one last picture. I saw myself being fused with the transfigured Christ and I could see His glorious body. As I walked up to people with demons they trembled at my feet because they recognized that I was one with Christ and they had to leave, I prayed for the sick and they were instantly healed. If you gain the revelation that you are one with Christ then you will begin to understand that you are hidden in Him, when you walk up to a person possessed by demons they see you but they also see that you are one with Christ and that you carry the authority and power of Jesus. I think that sometimes you can be so hidden in Christ that they get confused whether they are looking at you or Jesus and they can only do one thing, bow and leave at your command. Sickness and disease cannot stay in the presence of Jesus, it must leave when it sees Him and therefore it must listen to your commands. People will begin to see you differently as well because as you identify yourself with Him in the spirit you will become like Him in the natural. People will be overcome with the love and compassion that you carry.

Let me give you one last illustration that might help you to understand in a different way. Let's say that you are trying to build a house but a man with a couple of friends keeps coming by and destroying your work and mocking you. You feel powerless because it's just you versus a number of them. But then you meet someone and become really good friends, they happen to be a king with a large army of soldiers under their command. You continue building your house and the men come around again, however, this time your friend is with you and has a few hundred soldiers come out of hiding to surround the men. Who knows that even though you are standing there, those men are no longer seeing you, they are seeing the King and his soldiers and will turn around and run. This is what happens when you are in Christ and you pray for the sick or deliver someone. You lay hands on someone and the demons begin to manifest, you have no need to be afraid because you are one with Christ. Stand in faith, and in a moment, the demons will begin to see Christ and His army standing behind you. They will no longer see you because they will be overcome with fear of the one to whom you belong, the one with whom you are in relationship. When you give a command, the demons know that it carries the full backing of Christ and His power, authority and army, and they will obey because you are speaking on Christ's behalf.

There are other things that come along with this revelation. You are one with Him. Where is He right now? Seated in heavenly places. Where are you? Seated in heavenly places in Christ Jesus, you are one with Him, sitting on the throne next to the Father. This means you are *always* in His presence, you are constantly surrounded by His love, joy and peace. You never need to wonder. You always have access to these things, you just need to become aware of Him, become aware that you are one with Him and receive from Him. As you begin to understand this and walk in it, you now have the ability to live in perfect love, joy and peace in all circumstances. If depressing thoughts come your way, take them to the presence of the throne and replace them with peace. You only ever need to turn your attention to Jesus and He will give you what you need.

You are Fearless

Fear is the number one driving force behind why people are not operating in the supernatural, and not understanding their identities. If you completely understand who you are in Christ then His perfect love casts out all the fear. This is one of the biggest and most important journeys that we can undertake, and also one of the most challenging.

I was watching a movie called the Green Lantern the other day which has an awesome contrast between the power of fear and faith. This guy is chosen to be a guardian of the earth and his job description is to be fearless. He is told that a guardian is never chosen by mistake and there is something in him that he cannot see yet. He still thinks that he is full of fear and his girlfriend comes to him and says this, "I can see what they see, they didn't see that you had no fear they saw that you have the ability to overcome fear, you are courageous." This reminded me of when the disciples in Acts had just been put in jail and flogged. They came out and had a prayer meeting asking God to stretch out His hand and perform miracles and heal the sick. Acts 4:29-31. This was the very thing for which they had been imprisoned, however they also prayed for boldness or courage to proclaim the gospel. We don't need to struggle with fear, however if we still do, we can turn to God and ask Him to give us His courage and love to overcome.

Eventually I believe there is a place where we don't need to live with fear in our lives. You don't ever see Jesus being afraid, in Timothy 1:9 it says "we have not been given a spirit of fear but of power, love and a sound mind." In Romans 8:15 it says "For you have not received a spirit of slavery leading to fear again, but you have received a spirit of adoption as sons by which we cry out, "Abba! Father!" You can see through scripture that fear is actually a spirit, we don't need to partner with this spirit or agree with it. We can tell it to leave because it doesn't belong to us, and we can partner with the spirit of peace, love and courage.

Ultimately we need to die to our self and realise we are alive in Christ. If you walk up to a dead body at a funeral you can do anything you like but you will not be able to put fear into that person, why? Because they are dead. This is the way we should be to the fear of man, there is absolutely nothing that they can do to us.

So what has been my journey with breaking fear? Honestly I am still walking this one out however I have come a long way. When I first went to Bethel I was very insecure and I was afraid of man, I was always thinking about what everyone else was thinking about me. You cannot and will not live for God if you are always concerned with what other people are thinking about you. God gently began breaking fear off my life. Firstly He showered me with His love and established my foundation as His son whom He completely loves. I know that I am loved and accepted by my Father and no one can change that. You see one of my biggest fears was not being accepted, of being rejected and not being loved. This was because I was trying to gain my acceptance and my love from the world instead of receiving it from God. If I know how much He loves me and accepts me, it frees me from the world because it doesn't matter what they think about me, it only matters what He thinks about me.

I was in worship shortly after I arrived in Bethel and God said "Jason put your hands in the air and worship me." I said, "but God there are all these people around, they are going to be watching me." He said, "are you here to worship me or to receive worship from man? I need to be your only focus when you worship. Worship is just about you and me. There is no one else in the room except the two of us." Although it felt very strange I raised my hands in the air, out of obedience, and worshipped Him. When I did He met me and hit me with His love, His power and His freedom. It took time, but every time I was obedient to do what God told me to do I would feel fear lose a bit more of its grip on my life and I would walk into a little more freedom.

I was in Nebraska one time and Ruth who was my leader said she wanted us to ask God what He wanted us to do and then to be obedient. So during worship I asked the Lord what to do and he said "there is an angel standing on the stage with his back to the audience and his hands raised, I want you to go and stand on the stage in the exact position of the angel and raise your hands in worship." This thought absolutely terrified me, however I knew it was God and I wanted to be obedient. So I walked up the front jumped on the stage and stood where He told me to with my back to the church and my hands raised. As soon as my hands went in the air I was hit by the love of God and I began to weep and I ended up on my face on the stage. However, at the same moment He released me from another huge dose of fear of man and I walked into more freedom than I had ever experienced.

One of my biggest fears was dancing in front of people. One worship time in school the Holy Spirit was going wild and everyone was going crazy and doing what they were told. I was in my seat and Holy Spirit said "it's time to break the fear of dancing, go up the front onto the stage in front of nine hundred people and start dancing for me." This one was a battle but in the end I obeyed and went to the front on the stage and started dancing and again was met with incredible fear breaking freedom.

It is only in situations like these that you have the opportunity to use God's courage to step into freedom. In your own power you will not be able to break this fear, however, through His strength you can do anything. You can never walk into freedom while remaining comfortable, which is why so many people remain in bondage to fear. You are probably realising by now that the one constant thing that allowed me to break the barrier of fear in my life was listening to the voice of the Holy Spirit, it is intimacy with Him and obedience to His voice that will set you free. When He tells you to do something He will give you the strength and the courage to do it, if you will yield to Him and allow Him to work through you.

Another one of my all-time biggest fears was open air preaching, so one day at treasure hunting they told me I was going to open air preach. We went down to a local bus stop and there were six people waiting for a bus. My leader went out and introduced me saying I was going to give them some good news, and then I walked out and preached the gospel to these people and again shattered more fear off my life.

You begin to ask yourself each time why was I so afraid? There was actually nothing to be afraid of. If people reject me on the streets they aren't actually rejecting me they are rejecting God because I'm approaching them as His ambassador. I don't take their rejection personally. I used to, and it got really depressing and I wanted to give up approaching people. My first day out on the streets I got rejected by the first 6 people I approached and I wanted to quit. But then I realised the rejection wasn't mine to take and I allowed God to take it for me. My only job is to love the person who is in front of me and to allow them to encounter the love of Jesus through me. So now rejection just slides right off me and can't get attached.

My sole audience is Jesus Christ and Him alone. I do nothing to entertain or to make men or women happy, my full focus and attention is doing what pleases God. So bringing this into relation with healing – when you see someone and you feel like you should approach them instantly the devil starts whispering in your ear a million lies. What if they reject you? What if people see you get rejected then it will be even more rejection and people will think I'm a fool. What if I pray for them and they aren't healed? If you wait long enough you will talk yourself out of praying for the person. Believe me I know I have talked myself out of praying for many people. I have learnt that the quicker you respond to the prompting of the Holy Spirit the easier it is to see breakthrough.

So next time these thoughts come your way, and believe me they will, think about these answers instead. Who cares if they reject you? Your acceptance isn't found in man it's founded in God, He loves and accepts you and will get so super excited if you would trust Him and take a step of faith. If you approach them and get rejected, God will still be over the moon pleased with you. Who do you want to please people or your Father? Anyway they aren't rejecting you they would be rejecting Him. *But* what if they don't reject you? What if they have been asking God if He is real because they are contemplating suicide that day and you approach them with the love of Jesus and pray for them and they get healed in their body, set free from the spirit of suicide and give their lives to Christ? The only way to know is to take that leap of faith and ask. *No one has ever become great by staying on the sidelines.* So how about next time you turn your attention to what could happen and not what might not happen. We need to live a lifestyle of worship, where our entire lives revolve around just me and Him and doing whatever He tells us to do whenever He tells us to do it knowing that He has our best in mind. There is no greater joy than obedience to the King.

Humility

Jesus gives us the keys to his ministry in John 5:19-20 "Jesus gave them this answer: "Very truly I tell you, the Son can do nothing by himself; he can do only what he sees his Father doing, because whatever the Father does the Son also does. 20 For the Father loves the Son and shows him all he does."

Let me break this down for you. Firstly, Jesus shows us incredible humility and how we can walk in humility by realising that he could do nothing of himself, **Jesus the son of God was completely dependent on His Father and the Holy Spirit for any power to operate in His life.** If you want to cultivate a life of power, then ask the Lord for humility and humble yourself before Him. **Recognise that you are not the source of power, He is, and you can do nothing without Him.** Dependence on God is a key to walking in Humility.

Secondly, Jesus knew His identity as the Son of God and knew that the Father loved Him which is why He would show Him all things. We need to spend time with our Father and allow Him to establish our identity as sons and daughters. We need to know that we are totally loved by the Father and therefore He wants to share all things with us as well.

Thirdly, Jesus knew His Father, and had a deep intimate relationship with Him. This didn't just happen because He was Jesus, He spent a lot of time developing this relationship with His father. Luke 5:16 reads, "But Jesus often withdrew to lonely places and prayed." He would take time away to spend communing with the father.

James 4:6 "God resists the proud, but gives grace to the humble." One of the most important things to remember when praying for the sick, or when ministering, is that you can do nothing without Him. You are completely dependent upon Him. By this I mean that you can only heal the sick in relationship with Jesus. Everything that we do is by the grace of God: it is through His unmerited favour, goodness and kindness that He allows us to be used to bring Him glory. You remain in His flow of grace by staying humble, and you stay humble by remembering that you can do nothing without His grace.

I know better than anyone else, that without Christ I cannot heal the sick, I cannot know intimate details about people's lives and I cannot tell people their futures. Only God knows these things, and it is a very humbling experience when He uses you to release this type of information to people, or when you have the privilege of seeing a sick person healed. Always remember that you cannot heal the sick and that it is an incredible honour and privilege to be used by Him. He doesn't need someone powerful or intelligent, He just needs someone who is willing to be yielded to Him, through whom He can flow. The more you understand that you can do nothing without Him, the more you will minister out of a place of rest, because the pressure is off you.

However, you will also understand the importance of your personal relationship with the Holy Spirit; that He is the one who is doing all the miracles through you. Make sure that He receives the glory when the miracles take place. You see, I know that I do not deserve to be used by God. The number of times I have failed Him, and He has picked me up, forgiven me, and empowered me by His Grace, are endless. However I also understand that I am worthy and qualified to be used by Him because of His blood and the price that He paid.

You see false humility is just as bad as pride. Lots of people say I'm not worthy to be used. *No*, you *weren't* worthy to be used *but* the blood of Jesus made you worthy and qualified you. However make sure you don't walk in an entitlement spirit. You can be used because of His blood, but always remember that it was His price, and it is His power, that flows through you. Humble yourself and exalt the name of Jesus at all times: don't worry about the fear of man, but fear the Lord.

You are a servant son, your identity is as a son, your mission is to serve. Part of your relationship with the Lord is working out who you are alive to serve. You aren't here to serve yourself, to gain a name or reputation for yourself. The anointing and favour on your life has a purpose. Your job is to discover the purpose of the favour and then use that favour to serve the people you are called to serve. The anointing is not to serve yourself, it has a purpose. Jesus understood His identity as the Son of God, but He also understood His mission was to serve. He was a servant leader and a servant king, and He was a humble leader. Most of the world thinks this means He was weak because humility is weakness, however, Jesus shows us that humility is actually strength. Pride is much weaker than humility, humility is much harder to walk in than pride. It develops, creates and requires a greater level of strength to live a life of humility.

Philippians 2:3-11 "Do nothing out of selfish ambition or vain conceit. Rather, in humility value others above yourselves, not looking to your own interests but each of you to the interests of the others. In your relationships with one another, have the same mindset as Christ Jesus: Who, being in very nature God, did not consider equality with God something to be used to his own advantage; rather, he made himself nothing by taking the very nature of a servant, being made in human likeness. And being found in appearance as a man, he humbled himself by becoming obedient to death— even death on a cross! Therefore God exalted him to the highest place and gave him the name that is above every name, that at the name of Jesus every knee should bow, in heaven and on earth and under the earth, and every tongue acknowledge that Jesus Christ is Lord, to the glory of God the Father."

There are two main points that leap out at me from this scripture to teach us about humility. The first is in verse 6 He did not consider equality with God something to be used to His own advantage. Jesus knew His identity and His position in the kingdom, however, the key here is that He didn't use it for His own advantage. He used His position as a tool to serve those around Him, not to serve Himself. Humble people will use their position of power or influence to empower others and to serve others. They won't use that position for their own gain, but will recognise they are in that position for others.

The second point is in verse 8 it says He humbled Himself *by* being obedient to a cross. In this verse He tells us exactly what humility looked like in the context of Jesus life. Humility looks like obedience. Humble people will be obedient to the voice of God. They will choose to do what He tells them to do no matter what anyone else says.

True humility is a position of the heart – you know your identity, and you know your value, and you know that you aren't any better than anyone else in the room, and you know everyone else's value. When you truly understand your value, then you will have no problem serving and valuing others. Which means that part of walking in humility is recognising your identity and value.

Humility can take many different forms, let me use two characters in the Bible to explain how humility operated in their lives. The first person I'd like to look at is Paul.

I would say that Paul modelled humility among the apostles and we can learn a lot from his life about how humility operates. Paul was dependent upon God and he knew and recognised his weaknesses. In 2 Corinthians 12:9-10 he actually links weakness with power. "But he said to me, my grace is sufficient for you, for my power is made perfect in weakness. Therefore I will boast all the more gladly about my weaknesses, so that Christ's power may rest on me. That is why, for Christ's sake, I delight in weaknesses, in insults, in hardships, in persecutions, in difficulties. For when I am weak, then I am strong." When you have a revelation that you are weak, it makes you realise your need for God. If you are strong then you don't need anyone to help you, however, if you recognise that you are weak in an area, then you recognise that you also require help in that area. Recognising your weaknesses makes you dependent on Christ, and allows His strength to operate through your life. Recognising this need and dependence on God is the building of humility.

I think Paul reveals something very powerful to us in 1 Timothy 1:13-16 "Even though I was once a blasphemer and a persecutor and a violent man, I was shown mercy because I acted in ignorance and unbelief. The grace of our Lord was poured out on me abundantly, along with the faith and love that are in Christ Jesus. Here is a trustworthy saying that deserves full acceptance: Christ Jesus came into the world to save sinners – of whom I am the worst. But for that very reason I was shown mercy so that in me, the worst of sinners, Christ Jesus might display his immense patience as an example for those who would believe in him and receive eternal life."

Paul lived a life of humility because he understood that he was the worst of sinners, however, he also knew that he was now redeemed and set free from that life of sin, and had become a son. He didn't forget that he was once a sinner who had been saved. His salvation was a point of humility, it was his deliverance that actually helped him to remain humble. You never need to dwell on the past and beat yourselves up for anything that you did in your past life, however, don't let yourself get so arrogant, self-centred and entitled, that you forget that once you were lost. Once you were a slave to sin and it's only because of the grace and the love of Jesus that you have been rescued from death, and now get to live in righteousness. As a believer you should have compassion for a lost world and be longing for every person to encounter Jesus. Humility is a launching pad for evangelism, it also leads us into a recognition of a deeper need for relationship with Jesus which we will now cover in the next section of this book.

Intimacy

Developing intimacy with the Lord is a major key to Cultivating a Life of Power.

Importance of Intimacy

I learned a lesson in April 2013 when I went on a mission trip to Mexico City. It is, to this day, my favourite mission trip, I saw more miracles and salvations in one week than I had in my entire life. My dreams came true: I was stuck standing on a street corner for 4 hours praying for the sick and watching a minimum of 40 people being healed and people giving their lives to Jesus. I saw two ladies paralysed down the right side of their bodies, with pain through their entire bodies completely healed and restored. I saw deaf ears open and blind eyes see, tumours dissolve and hundreds of people saved, but during that week I still felt as though I was missing something.

There was a tug on my spirit and I just wasn't satisfied. I was wondering about it during the week but I was enjoying myself so much I didn't have all that much time to ask God. I would go home and write down the testimonies and thank Him for everything that had happened and then fall asleep. Somewhere near the end of the trip I had time with the Lord and I asked Him about what I was feeling. He led me to this scripture. Matt 7:22 "You cast out demons in my name, you healed the sick in my name and *I never knew you,*" (emphasis added) and it grieved my heart. God is always gentle with you and will never tell you something that you aren't ready to receive. I always wondered how this scripture could be fulfilled. Now I'm sure this scripture has many meanings, but let me tell you what I feel like God was saying to me. I had become so focussed on all the amazing miracles that God was doing, and I was so busy doing the work for God, that I had no time to spend with Him.

God does not desire for us to work for Him, He desires for us to know Him intimately. He wants us to know His heart and to spend time with Him. I realised that week that you can see thousands of miracles, hundreds of salvations but they will never satisfy you, *only* intimacy with Jesus will ever satisfy you.

Never get too busy doing work for God that you don't spend time with Him. Knowing God is not about spending time with Him for a day and then working for Him for two weeks and coming back to Him. Knowing God is living in intimacy on a daily basis, including Him in every aspect of your life, loving Him and receiving His love every morning and every night, and communing with Him during the day. He wants to know you, and more than anything He wants you to know Him.

God's Invitation

God is extending an invitation to you today to develop greater intimacy with Him, to go deeper into His heart. I was in worship recently, just spending time with the Lord, and I asked if He had anything to show me. I felt His call to go deeper, and saw a picture of flash lights. I asked the Lord what He was saying and He said "Jason they aren't flash lights they are search lights." I heard the scripture, Psalm 139:23-24 "Search me, God, and know my heart; test me and know my anxious thoughts. See if there is any offensive way in me, and lead me in the way everlasting." I said "God I give you permission to search me and to know me completely" and this was the startling and powerful moment for me. I heard the voice of God so clearly instantly respond "Jason you have permission to search my heart and to know me completely".

You see true intimacy is not just God knowing about *your* heart but *you* knowing *His* heart.
Intimacy is a two-sided coin. In my relationship with my wife, I spend time pursuing her and getting to know her heart and her desires, and she also pursues me and spends time getting to know my heart. If I was the only one pursuing her heart then it wouldn't be intimacy. We don't develop intimacy with God by Him alone pursuing our heart, we develop intimacy as we realise that He is pursuing us and we then turn our attention to pursuing His heart. It is the pursuit of each other's heart that develops intimacy. This invitation is being extended to you right now as you read this book. Accept it and go deeper with Him. Be still and know that He is God, give Him permission to search your heart and accept God's invitation to search His.

David surrendered his heart in this passage and gave God permission to search his heart and to know everything about him. Something powerful takes place in your relationship with God when you begin to give Him permission to move in your life. Does God need your permission to do things? No, however, because He is such a relational God He doesn't want to force Himself on you. My pastor, Tony Scown, always says "God doesn't want to be shoved down people's throats, He wants to be accepted into their hearts." The point being, that everything God does He does through relationship, and everything He does is to grow deeper in intimacy with you and me.

Even the way God speaks to us, is for the benefit of intimacy. In the above example you will see that God spoke to me through pictures and this is one way that God can speak. Why does He speak through pictures or dreams? Why does He use parables in the scriptures? Because every time I see a picture or have a dream, it gives me an opportunity to take it back to God, spend more time with Him and allow Him to translate it for me and teach me more about Himself. Proverbs 25:2 "It is the glory of God to conceal a matter; to search out a matter is the Glory of kings." God has orchestrated everything to develop deeper intimacy with you and the power of God flows through sons and daughters who have an intimate relationship or connection with their father.

Importance of Worship

David was a man after God's own heart and the key to David's life was his heart of worship. The key to true worship is surrender of the heart. Many believe that worship is simply standing in church singing songs to God. This isn't the case! If worship does not come from your heart then it's not worship, it's just singing a song. Worship is a heart to heart connection with God. *True* worship is a *response* to seeing Jesus, becoming aware of Him. Aware of His peace, goodness and His faithfulness; of seeing the price He paid for you and all He accomplished on the cross for you. Remember in the book of Revelation it says the creatures are around the throne and they are crying "Holy, Holy, Holy" all the time in worship. Did you know that they aren't getting tired, they aren't getting worn out, they aren't trying to worship? They look at Jesus and see something they've never seen before and automatically respond in worship, "Holy", then they look again and see something brand new about His nature and respond in worship for all eternity, responding to the greatness of God. You can't *try* to worship, you can never truly worship from a place of striving. Here's the thing though, to have this connection with God, and then to maintain it, requires a lifestyle of surrender. Paul explains this in Romans 12:1 "Therefore I urge you, brethren, by the mercies of God, to present your bodies a living and holy sacrifice, acceptable to God, *which is* your spiritual service of worship." What is your spiritual service of worship? To present your body as a living and holy sacrifice. This means to live a life surrendered to God. David understood the power of worship. Worship releases revelation which causes transformation and breakthrough.

Since worship is the response of your heart, worship requires you to open your heart to see God, as you experience God He releases revelation which creates healing and allows you to surrender your heart even more, creating intimacy. Therefore, the direct result of worship is intimacy with God, as your heart connects more deeply with Him and He reveals more and more about who He is, what He has done and who He says that you are. As you see different aspects of God's heart, your heart begins to be transformed. I'll share a story from my life as an illustration of how this has worked for me.

During worship one day I was encountering the presence of God and the congregation got stuck on the song "Holy, Holy, Holy" and we just kept singing it over and over again. As we were encountering the holiness of God I saw what was happening in the spirit. Every time we declared "Holy," His holiness was being released upon us to change us to become like Him. His Holiness was pouring over us every time we sang "Holy," and it seemed violent like an act of war. I realised it was war, we were being changed to become the very thing we were declaring, but at the same time God's holiness was surrounding us as a force field and was waging war on our behalf. As we kept our eyes on Him and His holiness, the powers of darkness were being pushed back; with every declaration the darkness was being repelled. I realised this was the same with any attribute of God. As you see Him in His nature, and you declare how you see Him, you become like the very thing you are seeing and declaring. When you see God and He releases a revelation of His heart, as you declare that revelation, you are becoming more like Him.

Praise and worship are also your weapons of warfare. Once you learn this, it will change the way you fight. God has shown me many times the power of our worship as a weapon against the forces of darkness. I believe this will help you in your journey as it has helped me in mine. I have found that it is impossible to enter true worship and still hold onto things that are contrary to the spirit of Christ. Hebrews 13:15 "Through Jesus, therefore, let us continually offer to God a sacrifice of praise—the fruit of lips that openly profess his name." Have you ever wondered why it is called a sacrifice of praise? A sacrifice means you are giving up something. You need to sacrifice to live a surrendered life. Generally, a sacrifice means that you don't want to do something, but you do it anyway. This is actually a real key to living a life of victory and overcoming the enemy. It's okay to offer a sacrifice of praise. I don't know about you but when I'm having bad thoughts, when the enemy is coming against my mind with stress, anxiety, depression or any other attack, the last thing I want to do is praise God, even though I know that is my source of victory. And for me, when I used to begin thinking about praising God, I would hear the voice of condemnation telling me that I was a hypocrite and I was being fake. If you have heard those lies, or if you still hear those lies, let me free you. They are lies of the enemy attempting to stop you from praising God, because the enemy knows that if you begin offering a sacrifice of praise, he is going to lose his hold on you, and you will enter freedom. I promise you I have had some bad days. One day my friend's baby, for whom we had been praying, died, and I was struggling big time. The enemy was screaming at me, and I knew my victory would be found in worship, but it was the last thing I wanted to do. The Holy Spirit prompted me to offer a sacrifice of praise. So I began to offer a sacrifice of praise and believe me it was a sacrifice. However, as I started praising God by faith, it wasn't long before I entered into worship. Why does it tell you to offer a sacrifice of praise? Because as you begin to praise Him, you start to become aware of Him and you begin to gaze upon Him; and as you start to see Him, you enter into worship, because now you aren't in a place of trying to praise God you are responding to Him. God responds to faith. If you don't feel like worshipping, then start to praise by faith. This activates God's grace to work on your behalf. It moves your eyes from your problem to the answer; your attention is being drawn to Christ and He begins to open your heart. The sacrifice of praise gives God an opportunity to encounter you and set you free. It is impossible for you to hold onto anything if you want to move into worship.

You need to surrender everything in your heart and as you do, He takes you and reveals Himself to you, and your heart begins to respond in worship. In this place of worship, you are completely surrendered to Him. No depression, no anxiety, stress, anger, nothing can remain as you worship because you've had to let it all go, and He delivers you and releases you of your burdens. I strongly encourage you: don't let the enemy steal your victory if you are having a bad day, offer a sacrifice of praise and see what God will do.

I heard a minister once share this exercise and it helped me. He said when you are having depressive thoughts or a bad day, lift up your voice and yell at the top of your lungs hallelujah 5 times and see what happens. I challenge you right now, if you are having a bad day, to stop and yell hallelujah at the top of your voice. Hallelujah means "I will exalt the Lord." You are telling your soul to exalt the Lord, and as you do, you can no longer hold onto the negative thoughts.

One day I was driving in the car and I was having a bad day. It just seemed like everything was going wrong and mentally I was heading to a bad space. Suddenly I heard the Holy Spirit say, "it's time to Warship." I thought what is that? And He said, "it's time to do war with your worship," So I began praising God in the midst of my circumstances, declaring who He is and how great He is, and as I did His presence filled the car and delivered me, and freed me.

Another time I was in worship and I heard the Holy Spirit say, "would you like to know what spiritual warfare looks like?" I said, "yes." He said, "open your eyes," I opened my eyes and looked around and I saw 900 revivalists with their hands in the air, adoring and worshipping Jesus. He said, "this is what spiritual warfare looks like, resting in my presence, adoring and worshipping me." He showed me a picture of our praise and worship going into the heavens like missiles, destroying demonic strongholds. He said, "what does the devil want? He wants your worship. In everything he does he is trying to get you to worship him, so the most powerful act of warfare you can do is when he is trying to get your full attention, which is worship to him, you simply choose to turn all of your attention to me and begin to adore me, praise and worship me and this will destroy the power of the enemy."

I have seen very many times in my life, that as I turn my attention to the Lord and worship Him, the powers of darkness lose all of their power in those circumstances and are defeated every time. Worship pushes back the darkness that is around you, and releases the light and glory of the Lord which becomes a shield. One last example just occurred as I was writing this. My friend has had a hard time this week, so I spent a few minutes to pray for him. As I began praying, I saw myself standing around him in the spirit. I saw hordes of the enemy coming against him and I had a sword to fight. This is normal for me. I'm a warrior so I love to fight, however in this instance the Lord had something different in mind. He simply told me to raise my hands over my friend and begin to sing "How Great is our God," so that is what I did. I raised my hands and began to sing 'How Great is our God." As I began to sing, I saw a portal from heaven open up over my friend, and the glory of the lord shone down upon him. It was such a warm and incredible golden presence, and as it was released, the darkness disappeared; it simply couldn't stand in the presence of God. The worship released the glory, which defeated the enemy.

David lived a lifestyle of worship, it wasn't something he did, it was who he became. We need to be living in this same heart-posture of worship. We need to be consciously aware of Jesus at all times, and then you will stay in a place of responding to Him in worship throughout your day. I guarantee your life will change effortlessly.

I want to ask you a question. How would you worship if you were standing in the throne room of God staring into the eyes of Jesus? Would you be striving? Would you be looking around worrying about what other people are thinking about you, or why people are walking in late etc.? No. You would be responding in worship to Him. Another question. Do you know that is actually your reality? This is what I believe God wants to say, "next time you come to church, find your seat, then close your eyes and become aware of the reality that you are actually, right that second, standing in the throne room before Jesus. If you can't see anything, just believe by faith you are there. Take a couple of seconds to remind yourself how good He is and what He has done.

Then begin to respond to His goodness and worship Him face to face. If every person in the room began to operate in worship in this way, at the same time, I can't describe what God would begin to do.

To live this lifestyle of worship our hearts need to remain surrendered to the Lord. Let's take a look at surrender in the next chapter.

Importance of Surrender

I was in worship one day and I felt the Lord say, "there is a key in surrender". He didn't tell me what the key was, Proverbs 25:2 "It is the glory of God to conceal a matter; to search out a matter is the glory of kings." Sometimes He will give you a hint of a secret to see if you are hungry enough to seek after Him for the full revelation. He does this to develop deeper relationship with us.

For a while I have been searching for this key and, I believe, it is understanding what surrender means and what a surrendered life looks like. I'm going to attempt to explain how this looks. In most churches you have probably heard pastors and leaders talk about surrendering your life, surrendering everything. I don't know about you, but I have wondered what does that really mean? How do you practically surrender? What does it look like? I have been asking numerous people their perspectives; I put a question out on Facebook and had some great responses; I have been searching the scriptures, but it wasn't until I saw the demonstration of surrender in the life of my wife, that I actually had the revelatory moment.

One morning she woke up and was about to start work, when she decided that she was going to get some fresh air first and go for a bike ride to the shops. On her way there, she spotted an elderly man walking up a hill with a walking cane. Recently, she had prayed to be open for God to use her at any time as He wishes. She zoomed in on the man, very aware of his walking stick and thought to herself, "oh no what if God wants to use me now?" But she didn't have much time to decide as her bike was very quickly running down-hill. Undecided if she should stop to pray for the man, she slowed down her bike and said hello. He replied and stopped expecting her to continue the conversation. He was open, and so she proceeded to tell the man that she did itinerant ministry with her husband and have seen many healed, she then enquired what was wrong with his leg and if he would like the same healing touch for himself. He began tearing up and asked if she was a Christian and she said, "yes." He received prayer and told her that his leg felt much better and he felt tingles through it as she prayed. She prayed one last time to thank God for what he had already done and to bring complete restoration. The man left with a smile on his face and a well improved left leg. This is what a surrendered life looks like.

If I could sum up everything that I have learnt about surrender and give you my definition it would be this.

Surrender is to be open and willing to be moved by God when He speaks.

A surrendered life is one that is open and willing to allow God to move them anytime he wants in any area of their life. This requires a high degree of dying to yourself, obedience and sacrifice. It requires dying to yourself because very often He is going to ask you to do things that your flesh won't want to do. I think the best way to explain surrender is to give examples.

If you are carrying a burden and God asks you to give it to Him, surrender is to be willing to give that burden to Him. If He asks you to give a prophetic word or pray for someone sick, surrender is to be obedient to His voice and allow Him to move you. Jesus perfectly represented a surrendered life, He only did what He saw His Father doing. Every word He spoke was what He heard the Father speaking; He perfectly showed us a life of surrender, obedience and sacrifice. He gave up His will for the will of His Father: this was Jesus showing us what it looks like to die to yourself and live a surrendered life. Jesus had given His whole life to His Father, He was completely open to allowing God to move Him and ask Him to do anything and He would obey.

We need to allow God to do this in every area of our lives. He may ask us to give up mindsets, habits, dreams, desires, behaviours. Surrender is being obedient and allowing Him to make those changes in your life.

I found a journal entry from the 24th March 2013 that represents a day that I lived fully surrendered to the Lord. I believe this is the key God wanted to show me. One of the reasons Jesus had so much power manifest through His life, and affected so many people, was because He lived a surrendered life open for God to do anything.

"Today I had the opportunity to lead a small team in a small town called Fairbury, in a church of around 18 elderly people. We released three prophetic words each which were dead on, and had words of knowledge. I shared a quick message on power and released a bunch of testimonies then ran the ministry time.

Following prayer:

- *a lady with Parkinson's disease felt warmth in her back and she could sit and stand without help.*

- a lady with 2-3 years of neck and muscle pain had all that pain disappear
- a lady who described her pain as 11 out of 10 in her back had it disappear
- wrist pain from surgeries disappeared
- a lady's leg grew out and her back was almost completely healed
- a guy with pain in his knees, back and both shoulders frozen, had all the pain leave his knees and back, and there was more movement in both shoulders one more than another.

As you can tell there were quite a lot of people healed from a group of only 18 people: the power of God was really flowing.

It was a Pentecostal church and we found out, a couple of days before we were to attend the church, that the pastor had actually decided he didn't really want us to come. It was different from anything they had experienced before. We went out to Pizza Hut with the Pastor and his family after the service. I asked Sarah (a girl who was part of my ministry team) if she had a word for the waitress, so Sarah started prophesying over her. We asked if she had any pain and she said her shoulder was sore, so we asked the pastor's son to pray for her. It was a little better so we prayed again and she was completely healed. Then I asked, "Hey, do you know if anyone here has a problem with their right ankle?" and she said "how did you know that?" One of the guys she worked with had a problem with his ankle and she only got his number last night. We prayed for him and asked her to send him a text message. She did and he wrote back and said that his ankle was completely healed! Then I asked "does anyone have lower back pain?" and she said "you're good, how did you know that? I shouldn't be here today but I took the shift for Natasha who was suffering really bad back pain." This time the pastor's wife prayed with the waitress as a proxy, and asked her to text the girl Natasha.

Then I asked "does anyone on staff have migraines?" She said "I don't think so" and then another waitress Kate walked past and she said "Hey Kate do you have migraines?" And she said "yes why do you ask?" Kate came over, she was pregnant and had a headache 5 out of 10 pain. We got another guy who was with us to pray for her and all the pain left instantly so we prophesied over her as well. Ken was driving us home when his phone rang and instantly I got pain in my ear. They talked and when Ken hung up, the pain disappeared, so we called her back and asked if she had problems with her ears. She said she did not have pain but had problems with her hearing so I prayed for her.
I began to feel pain through my neck, ear and back of my head and felt it was for a

lady born near 1953. Ken said it was for one of his staff members and he would take me to his business to pray for her. They had a staff meeting that day and we arrived 15 mins after the meeting finished. The lady we were looking for was the only person that was still there and she was just about to leave the store. We pulled her back inside and I asked if she had a problem with her ear. She said she had a tumour in her ear and shingles on her face, we prayed for her and I saw the shingles disappear and she felt heat in her ear. Then we began prophesying over her and it was dead on and impacting. At the end I asked how she was feeling and her countenance had changed, she was touched and she was still feeling heat in her ear when she left.

Then I was still feeling pain in my neck so we asked God where we should go and we all felt like going to the coffee shop. We went and I asked both of the people behind the counter if they had pain in their neck and neither had any problems. Then a lady entered the store and Ken (our host) said Jason that's her she works here but she shouldn't be here today. I went over and asked her if she had stress headaches and she said yes and scoliosis so I started praying for her. God gave me a download about her and I started prophesying over her and sharing everything I saw and she began balling. I gave her a hug as she was crying heavily and I told her God loved her.

As we were leaving, a lady walked passed on crutches with something on her foot so I followed her back inside and talked with her. She had an infection in her foot. We got to pray for her and the first time nothing happened. The second time we prayed she felt a tingle and the third time she said that her foot was feeling a lot better than when we had started. She could put her foot on the ground and said there wasn't pain it was just tingling maybe a little tender. So we blessed her and left."

As you can see throughout this day we were totally open to hearing God's voice, and allowing Him to move us and do whatever He wanted, and power was flowing.

We need to surrender every area of our life. What does this mean? It means we need to focus on our relationship with the Lord and do whatever He says. We need to be open to Him correcting and discipling us, because of His love for us, and then accept and come into alignment with His adjusting.

I think part of the reason we don't surrender is because we don't understand why. As I said before, surrender means dying to self and accepting change. I don't know about you but I can be a little resistant to change sometimes, maybe you can relate to a conversation I had with the Lord. At one of these moments recently I told the Lord I don't like change and asked, "why is everything changing?" He responded, "Jason it's not that you don't like change it's that you don't like losing control, and the next season I'm asking you to give me control and surrender." He said, "if you really believed that I have a greater plan for your life than you do, then you would have no problem yielding to me and giving me control." He said "it really comes down to trust, how do you develop trust? You spend time getting to know someone. I'm calling you into deeper intimacy with me. Change is an invitation into a deeper relationship with me. Stop resisting change." He then showed me this picture and said, "it's like a caterpillar changing into a butterfly. If the caterpillar stayed in the cacoon and said, "no I refuse to change, I don't want to change. What's going to happen out there? What if my wings fail? What about all the enemies out there? I'll just stay here." This resistance would keep the caterpillar from experiencing the transformation and freedom of becoming a butterfly. The Lord said "by resisting change you will restrict your ability to fly to the places that I have called you to. As soon as you embrace my changes you will get your wings and fly to new heights, however the height you fly depends on the depth of intimacy you develop with me."

There is a very important season in the cacoon, this is where most of the change takes place. It can feel a little like a dentist chair. I went for a check-up recently and they told me I needed things done, I trusted the dentist and I actually *chose* to go back and asked him to work on me and fix anything that needed fixing, pull whatever needed pulling, restore whatever needed rebuilding and prevent future problems. I had a choice whether to go to the dentist or not to go. While I was being worked on, it was uncomfortable and occasionally painful. I had no idea what the dentist was doing, I was just trusting that throughout the discomfort everything would work out better in the end, because I believed the dentist had my welfare in mind. I could have stopped the dentist at any time and said, "hey no it's too uncomfortable, too painful, I'm leaving," and he would have let me go. However I *surrendered* to him and allowed him to do the work that needed to be done. We need to go to God and ask for a check-up, and then surrender to Him and allow Him to do whatever work is necessary, even if it's uncomfortable and a little bit painful, trusting that He has our best in mind and things will be better on the other side.

Part of the journey of living one with Christ is to lay yourself down, all your interests, all your desires, everything that is self-centred and focussed on yourself. You have to give up your will. If I give up my will then I can receive His will. Unless I let go I cannot receive; if I'm holding onto something then I am hindering myself from receiving something else. If I am holding a large rock in both my hands and then someone comes along and says would you like two large gold bricks, you would say, "yeah," but you're still holding the rocks. If you want the gold bricks you need to let go of the rocks to receive the bricks. We need to lay our will down, surrender to Jesus and receive His will for our life. Just like Jesus did in the Garden of Gethsemane when He said not my will but yours, Jesus was surrendering His will to the Father and He accomplished a lot more than He would have with His own will.

Often the journey of surrender can feel quite difficult. This is because you don't realise you have something to surrender until God challenges you to surrender it. Why does He ask you to do difficult things sometimes? To point out areas that we haven't fully surrendered yet. Surrender looks like something, if you surrender then your actions need to follow up. You can't just say, "I surrender my life," then Jesus says, "great move to Canada," and you say, "no way!" Your actions therefore show you aren't surrendered.

If you want to be used by God then you need to allow Him to do a work in you, and you need to be willing to live a life of surrender.

Connect to the Source

I was getting ready for a meeting one night where I was speaking on "Cultivating a Life of Power," and I asked the Lord how I could help people to walk in more power. He replied, "**Connect them to the source.** I am the source. I am the source of everything, if people want to walk in more power or miracles, signs and wonders *pursue me*."

If you have a laptop and it runs out of battery what do you need to do? Connect it to the power source, because if you keep the laptop continually plugged in to the wall then it will continually have power. This is the major key to successfully cultivating a life of power, constantly remain connected to the source of power. If the laptop is unplugged it can last a few hours, but then it becomes useless. The same thing occurs with us in our lives, we spend time with God, and then we go out and can operate in power. If we aren't continually connected to the source, then the power runs out and we need to go back and get refilled. The alternative is to remain constantly connected to the power source by living a life surrendered and submitted to God, being aware of His presence, and staying in communion with Him. This is how it is possible to live in divine health, if you touch the power of God then you will be healed, if you stay continually connected to the power of God, then you can live in divine health and see others healed.

This can be seen in scripture through John 15:5-8 "I am the vine; you are the branches. If you remain in me and I in you, you will bear much fruit; apart from me you can do nothing. 6 If you do not remain in me, you are like a branch that is thrown away and withers; such branches are picked up, thrown into the fire and burned.7 If you remain in me and my words remain in you, ask whatever you wish, and it will be done for you. 8 This is to my Father's glory, that you bear much fruit, showing yourselves to be my disciples."

Jesus says that He is the vine and we are the branches, He is the source into which we are plugged. Disconnected from the vine we can do nothing and will end up being thrown into the fire. However, if you remain connected intimately to Jesus and His words remain in you, (which is the importance of getting scripture into your hearts), then your heart will be shaped and conformed to His and your heart's desires will be His heart's desires. At this moment of oneness you can ask for anything you wish because it will line up with His will and it will be done for you.

1 John 5:14-15 "This is the confidence we have in approaching God: that if we ask anything according to his will, he hears us. And if we know that he hears us—whatever we ask—we know that we have what we asked of him."

You will have total confidence that God will answer your prayers because you know that you are praying in line with God's will and, according to 1 John 5, if you pray anything in accordance with His will then He hears you, and therefore, you know that you will have whatever you ask. This is why we can pray confidently when we are praying for the sick, because God has already clearly established in His word that it is His will to heal. Therefore, we are praying in accordance with His will, He hears us and will answer us.

John 15 Verse 8 is really important as well, it shows that God actually desires to answer our prayers, because through answering our prayers we bear much fruit, showing that we are His disciples and through doing so we bring glory to the Father. Would you like Jesus to be glorified through your life? Then pray prayers that only Jesus can answer and take part in things that only God can do. You can't heal the sick, therefore praying for the sick allows God to be glorified through your life, as you couldn't have done it in your own power.

Power will become the by-product of a life in surrender to Jesus, the by-product of a person who constantly pursues intimacy with Him. Right now the Lord is inviting you into a deeper place of intimacy with Him, not in church but alone at home in your secret place. **Don't hunger and thirst for miracles, hunger and thirst for Jesus and miracles will follow you.**

I promise you, He is waiting in your secret place to encounter you. The secret place is where most of your encounters will take place. Encounter creates transformation and transformed people transform cities and nations. Encounter comes through relationship, transformation comes through intimacy, every time you get closer to God you are being transformed. Matthew 6:6: "But when you pray, go into your room, close the door and pray to your Father, who is unseen. Then your Father, who sees what is done in secret, will reward you."

There is no shortcut to relationship or intimacy with the Lord. You need to spend time with Him. You need to lay your life at His feet and let Him search you and know you, and give Him permission to speak into your life to transform you. Pride works against God which is why He resists the proud but gives grace to the humble. Humble yourself before God and give Him permission to transform you. When He speaks, listen and be obedient, if He tells you to do something then do it.

Spend time in the secret place and get to know your Father, develop a relationship with Him. Ask Him questions and wait for the responses, allow Him to ask you questions and spend time listening to Him. **One word from God will transform you.**

Jesus said He only did what He saw the Father do and we must live in the same way, remaining close to the source and only saying and doing what He says and does. Let's take a look at a couple of scriptures. I'd like you to read these to discover how much time Jesus spent praying to the Father and building their relationship. These are just a few scriptures:

Mark 1:35 "Very early in the morning, while it was still dark, Jesus got up, left the house and went off to a solitary place, where he prayed."

Luke 11:1 reads, "One day Jesus was praying in a certain place."

Luke 5:16 reads, "But Jesus often withdrew to lonely places and prayed."

Luke 6:12" One of those days Jesus went out to a mountainside to pray, and spent the night praying to God.

Luke 5: Jesus *often* withdrew. This implies that He regularly withdrew from people to spend time praying. If Jesus, the Son of God, needed to spend time alone with the Father to hear His voice and to receive direction and instructions, it would seem logical that we would need to spend time alone with the Father. Wouldn't you agree? I don't care if you are in ministry, a lawyer, teacher or businessman or woman, would you like to be more successful and more fulfilled in life? If yes, then spend time aside, alone with the Father. Your satisfaction does not come from this world, nothing in the world will ever satisfy you, only Jesus.

The secret place is not just time alone, it's a position of the heart as we will see in the next chapter where we will go into more detail on how to build your secret place with the Lord.

Building your Secret Place

The secret place is not a particular location but a position of the heart, however, it often helps to get away from the busyness of life to focus on the Lord. How do you position yourself for encounter or how do you initiate an encounter? **A heart completely surrendered to Him positions itself for encounter.** Get hungry! You need to be desperate for change. You need to be ready and willing to change. You need to be ready to sacrifice your life, to sacrifice yourself, to surrender your will to His will, to humble yourself.

The more time you spend with God and experience Him, the more you want to experience Him and realise you need more of Him. You can actually tell how much time people are spending with the Lord based on how hungry they are for Him.

God said that what is done in secret will be displayed publicly. Matthew 6:6 "But when you pray, go into your room, close the door and pray to your Father, who is unseen. Then your Father, who sees what is done in secret, will reward you." This takes trust in the Lord.

There is no one whom I've met, walking in intimacy with Christ, who hasn't spent a huge amount time alone with God. You see them on stage or doing ministry but this is the overflow of their private life. What they do in public, the prayer meetings, the ministry, is an outflow; it is giving out of their secret place. If your secret place is dry then you have nothing to draw from. It's up to us personally to keep our fire burning, it's not the responsibility of our pastor, or our friends, or our wife, it's our personal responsibility to maintain and grow our relationship with the Lord.

It's easy to get passionate and on fire when we are in a prayer meeting with friends or in church. But what defines you, is when you go home and shut the door, how hungry are you in this place, when it's just you and God and no one is watching? Do you cry out for more, do you passionately pursue Him when no one else is around, when no one is watching or encouraging you, when you aren't told to pursue Him? Do you seek Him and delight yourself in Him?

As sons and daughters we need to be pursuing Him in private when no one else is watching. That's when you know you're hungry, and you are only doing it for Him and not for anyone else. If you are only getting filled up when you come to church, or when you are spending time with people, then what happens to your relationship with God if all the people leave? If your friends begin to persecute you or you get placed in jail; if you get sent to minister to a country where there are no other Christians? You should still be able to grow, but your growth will come from the hours you spend before the Lord, just you and Him.

It's similar to working out in the gym, you need hours a week to see any real growth in your body, and if you understand working out, then you realise that most of the growth occurs in the last 2 reps of any set that you do. It's these last couple of reps that create the transformation in your body. It's very easy to give up before these couple of reps, but if you do, you don't get the fullness of transformation. In the same way, it can be easier to give up in the secret place after an hour, or a week but let me encourage you, don't give up. It's when you feel like giving up that you know that transformation is just around the corner.

Some of my most defining encounters with the Lord are when I have been in my room alone crying my heart out. I've gotten down on my knees with my hands in the air, abandoned to Him, worshipping and crying out for more, or declaring His victory. Or when I've received breakthrough and I'm laughing for hours, just me and God, and He's whispering to me who I am and who He has created me to be. It's in this place that you encounter your provider, your healer, your strength, your refuge and shield. When you understand that He is your everything and He is all that you need. When you understand that if everything fails in life, and everyone turns against you, that He is more than enough for you.

The main function of the secret place is to grow in intimacy and build a closer relationship with God. This is where you access His face, His heart and where your identity and authority are established. This is the most crucial part of a Christian's life. The secret place requires honesty, transparency and trust. Let God search you and as you do, you will find safety and security in His presence.

Psalm 91:1 "He that dwelleth in the secret place of the Most High shall abide under the shadow of the Almighty."

Psalm 139:15 "My frame was not hidden from You, When I was being formed in secret, and intricately and skilfully formed [as if embroidered with many colours] in the depths of the earth."

So I've explained what the secret place is and for a long time I've heard many people and pastors talking about spending time in the secret place. However, I didn't actually know what that meant or what I was supposed to do when I got there. So now I'm going to talk about how to actually spend time there.

Like everything else this is a journey, and everyone's secret place will look different. I hope to give you some tools to use for yourself. However, this is not a formula. As you spend time with God He will create something unique between you and Him. Everything He does is for you to grow deeper in relationship with Him.

So you've shut your door and you are preparing to spend time with the Lord. What now? Honestly, sometimes it can feel strange, it can feel like you are praying to thin air, and like everything else in the kingdom, your secret place will require faith. You need to exercise faith that God is real and that you are spending time with Him even though you can't see Him. Hebrews 11:6 is the perfect scripture to demonstrate this, it says "And without faith it is impossible to please God, because anyone who comes to him must believe that he exists and that he rewards those who earnestly seek him." You need to start out believing that this is real. Exercising your faith to spend time alone with God pleases Him so much and He promises to reward those who seek Him. Jeremiah 29:13 "You will seek me and find me when you seek me with all your heart." God says that if you seek Him, you will find Him. Hold on to these promises, and Matthew 6:6 as quoted before, as you begin this journey in the secret place.

Be encouraged that it will, most likely, not always be like this. As you spend time with the Lord you do begin to see more in the spirit, you begin to feel His presence, encounter His peace, and hear His voice. It just takes time and faith. I used to begin by praying for everyone and everything I could think of and 15 mins later I'd be finished and wonder now what? Well the first thing to remember is that relationship takes time, you need to spend time with the Lord and He has given us many tools to use. We will discuss these tools in greater depth in the next chapter.

Tools to build the secret place

The secret place is where you grow with the Lord and it's also where you do battle with Him. He has given us tools, we use these tools to establish a depth of intimacy with Him. We can also use these tools in times of spiritual warfare as weapons against the enemy. Philippians 4 is a great chapter to study in the secret place, and it equips us with a number of tools we can use to build our secret place with the Lord. Let's take a look at a few of them:

Rejoicing
Philippians 4:4 "Rejoice in the Lord always. I will say it again: Rejoice!"
Paul emphasises the importance of rejoicing throughout all situations in life, and gives us a tool that we can use. Rejoice means to feel or show great joy or delight; the synonyms are happiness, pleasure, joy, delight, elation, cheer, jubilation, euphoria, ecstasy, rapture, exuberance, exultation, glory and delight to name a few. Spend time rejoicing before the Lord, dance, shout, clap your hands, be enraptured by Him, experience His joy, His pleasure for you, His delight in you, and then delight yourself back in Him.

Prayer, Petition, Thanksgiving
Philippians 4:6-7 "Do not be anxious about anything, but in every situation, by prayer and petition, with thanksgiving, present your requests to God. 7 And the peace of God, which transcends all understanding, will guard your hearts and your minds in Christ Jesus."
This gives us 3 tools – prayer, petition and thanksgiving, and all are slightly different. Prayer is any form of communicating with God, it's communing with Him. Petition is to humbly appeal, request or ask someone to act on behalf of a particular cause. Thanksgiving – is to give thanks. So this is how I would describe this passage and what it shows us about the secret place. Part of your time can be spent presenting requests to God on behalf of loved ones, friends, family or even particular situations in your own life. I see this time as intercession. However, this time will also include much thanksgiving and is done in the context of relationship with the Lord, spending time with Him.

Let me give you an example. I had a dream one night and I saw a person, who I knew, in a plane, and I watched as it crashed. The person was thrown from the plane and although people were shaken up, no one was seriously injured. I knew this was a warning that the person could potentially fall from ministry and people were going to be affected. I spent time with the Lord just spending time enjoying His presence communing with Him, and then I began thanking the Lord for this person and the call on their life, and thanking God for His goodness. I then presented a petition to the Lord that He might save this person from whatever temptation or mistake was going to come across their path and that He would look after the people who were around them, and then continued thanking the Lord for His plans and purposes over that ministry. This is how I see this scripture playing out in practice. Unfortunately, very shortly after that dream, it came true and there was a fall of that person. However, I believe that God's hand was on the situation and my prayers had made some sort of impact even though I didn't completely understand how.

Refocusing Your Thoughts
Philippians 4:8 "Finally, brothers and sisters, whatever is true, whatever is noble, whatever is right, whatever is pure, whatever is lovely, whatever is admirable—if anything is excellent or praiseworthy—think about such things." This is one of the most powerful scriptures and if you just spend time in the secret place adjusting to this one scripture, it would change your life. Paul is showing us a key, he's asking a question, "what are you focusing on?" What is your attention set on? We need to spend time recalibrating our thoughts to bring them in line with this scripture. Use this scripture to filter your thoughts. Bill Johnson says "we can't afford to have any thoughts in our heads that aren't in Jesus' head". If your thoughts aren't true, noble, right, pure, lovely, admirable, excellent or praiseworthy then adjust your thoughts to those that are. I consider this to be a form of spiritual warfare that you can do in the secret place.

Meditation
It also brings up another tool which is that of meditation. Now I know lots of people are afraid of meditation but there is great power in true Biblical meditation. Joshua 1:8 "Keep this Book of the Law always on your lips; meditate on it day and night, so that you may be careful to do everything written in it. Then you will be prosperous and successful."

The occult and eastern religions use meditation because of its power, however they say that meditation is to empty your mind. This is dangerous. True Biblical meditation is actually the opposite, meditation is to fill your mind with the word of God and then to chew on it, mull over it, ponder, contemplate, consider and think over the scripture continually. Meditate on the word, grab a scripture such as Philippians 4:5 "The Lord is near." Now repeat that to yourself over and over and over during the day, let your heart open to the reality that the Lord is near. What does that feel like? What does it look like? Once you have spent time chewing on it, and have received a heart revelation of the word, ask the Lord for another verse. This is a very powerful tool for us to utilise in our time with the Lord.

Praying in Tongues
This is one of the most powerful tools that God has equipped believers with and many are not utilising because they don't understand it. Both John G Lake and Smith Wigglesworth attributed a large portion of the power they walked in, to praying in tongues on a regular basis. This is because they understood what was taking place as they were praying. I believe that many people don't understand why they should be praying in tongues, or what happens when they do.

Here are a few verses talking about praying in tongues. In 1 Corinthians 14:18 Paul says that he thanks God that he prays in tongues more than all of them. He also mentions in 1 Corinthians 14:2 "For anyone who speaks in a tongue does not speak to people but to God. Indeed, no one understands them; they utter mysteries by the Spirit." In verse 4 he says "Anyone who speaks in a tongue edifies themselves". 1 Jude 20-21 "But you, beloved, building yourselves up on your most holy faith, praying in the Holy Spirit, 21 keep yourselves in the love of God, waiting anxiously for the mercy of our Lord Jesus Christ to eternal life."

Obviously, Paul prayed in tongues a fair bit and understood how important it was. One of the fruits of praying in tongues is revelation as can definitely be seen through the life of Paul. He also says that "tongues" is not talking to humans but to God and it isn't for edification of the body but edification of yourself. This is confirmed in Jude when it says to build up your most holy faith by praying in the spirit, it then says that another benefit of praying in the spirit, is that you will be keeping yourselves in the love of God. Would you like a deeper revelation of the love of God? Pray in tongues.

Let me give you my definition of praying in tongues. Tongues is applying your faith, to surrender control, to allow the Holy Spirit to speak through you. Why would you want to do this? I gained this revelation of the power of speaking in tongues in 2013 while reading a book that I would highly recommend, by Dave Roberson, called "Walking in the spirit, walking in power". This is the revelation on tongues that I had. The Holy Spirit is a person and He is God. He also now lives in you once you accept Jesus as your Lord and saviour. If the Holy Spirit is God, then it means that He wasn't created, He has *always* existed and is outside of time. The Holy Spirit was part of the planning process to create you. He helped to imagine you, He helped to plan your purpose, your call, your destiny, to order your steps, to create the works that you were going to walk in. This means He knows who you are created to be, and He knows what you need to become who He created you to be.

Let me ask you a question; next time you are in your secret place, would you like to pray your perfect prayers over what you think your destiny and call is, and what you think the will of God is for your life? Or would you like to yield yourself to the Holy Spirit through faith and allow Him, *God* the Holy Spirit, to pray on your behalf His perfect will for your life, to pray His purpose and destiny over your life, to build you up in faith, to edify you and encourage your spirit? I know which one I would choose. When I gained this revelation you couldn't stop me praying in tongues, and I can tell you it is powerful and it changes you. You are no longer hindering God from transforming you, but are yielding and allowing the Holy Spirit to do the work in you that He knows needs to be done.

In 1 Corinthians 14:14 it says "For if I pray in a tongue, my spirit prays, but my mind is unfruitful." This is because your mind doesn't understand what your spirit is praying. This actually provides you with an opportunity, because as you pray in tongues with your spirit you can be focusing your mind on Christ as well.

I want you to try a few things with me. Right now, I'm going to have you pray in tongues for a minute naturally, not focusing, just praying. You can do this all day, while you are doing any number of things throughout the day, and it will bring you great fruit. This will be building and edifying yourself and is fruitful for your spirit.

Now I want you to pray a minute in tongues, eyes shut, focusing on your spirit pressing into the Spirit of God. I see my spirit actually moving forward into the presence of God and I recognise the glory that is around me. As I'm praying in tongues, I'm pressing into His glory, using my imagination and focusing on praying in the spirit. Could you feel the difference? Whenever you have a chance, while praying in tongues, shift your attention to His presence and His glory, and it will take you deeper and will be even more powerful.

Praying in Tongues While Reading the Bible

You can also pray in tongues while reading scripture at the same time. I've found this really powerful, considering when you pray in tongues your mind is fruitless. Therefore, if you take a passage of scripture and read it 5 or 6 times while praying in tongues, it feels as though your spirit is opened wider to receive revelation about the word. I also pray in tongues while listening to the sermon in church or podcasts while at home, it opens my spirit to be more sensitive to hear the word of God. My spirit is praying and receiving the words being released, while my mind is taking in the message. You don't need to pray loudly, it's not about volume; you can even pray in your head or under your breath. You can also meditate on scripture in your mind while praying in tongues. All of these are powerful tools you can use during your time with the Lord.

Be Still

Psalm 46:10 "Be still and know that I am God." This is another powerful tool you should be using, just being completely still and silent before the Lord and allowing Him to encounter you in whatever way that looks in the moment. Just be still and know or experience that He is God. You have to build this silent time into your secret place.

Worship

Worship is another great tool to establish intimacy with the Lord.

So what's next? How do you actually engage with the presence of God? How do you enter into His presence and how do you initiate an encounter?

How to Initiate Encounter

Firstly, you need to know that God has already done His part: He has already sent His son, and when Jesus died the veil was torn as a symbol that we now have unlimited access through Jesus to the Holy of Holy's. The Father is waiting for you to seek Him and initiate an encounter. I had this picture one time: I saw the Father sitting in the throne room and then I saw a person sitting in their bedroom. The person was praying really hard to encounter God, to see God, to rend the heavens and tear the veil, and there was a closed door in front of them. On the other side of that door was the Father sitting on His throne with His arms open wide and He was lovingly, longing for the person to realise that He had already rent the heavens, and had already torn the veil, and He was ready to encounter the person. My perspective changed and I began to see everything from the Father's perspective on the throne. As He looked at the person, there was no door, no veil, nothing stopping the person from the encounter they were longing for except their own mindset.

This changed my perspective and I realised that I was that person and actually there was nothing stopping me right this second from encountering the Lord. There is no veil, there is no door; God doesn't need to rend the heavens because He's already done it when Christ came. In Christ I'm already seated in heavenly place and I already have access to the spirit realm, I just need to accept it, believe it, and then position my heart in this truth. Initiating an encounter is as simple as believing that God wants to encounter you. God sent Jesus to die so that you could encounter Him and have relationship with Him. Shut your eyes, believe that God is waiting to encounter you and then realise you're already in His presence.

Here are some more practical tools to help you position your heart to encounter God. Ultimately encountering God is about positioning your heart to see, hear and experience Him. I believe this is what Chronicles is referring to in 1 Chronicles 16:11 when it says to seek His face continually and in 1 Chronicles 22:19 where it says to "Now set your heart and soul to seek the Lord your God". To seek and pursue God is to set your heart's desire and affection towards Him, believing that He wants to encounter you. Unless you have the belief that God desperately wants to encounter you as much as you want to encounter Him, you won't have the faith or motivation to pursue Him. You need to know that God rewards those who diligently seek Him. Let's look at some practical ways to position your heart to seek the Lord.

How to enter the presence:

- Have **worship music** playing either with or without words, it's up to you. Worship brings an atmosphere of heaven, and invites the angelic, as they love to worship and to watch you worship. Worship brings peace, love and joy into your atmosphere, and allows you to still your heart and focus your heart's attention on the Lord. I have worship music playing as much as possible throughout the day, and when I have quiet time with the Lord I always begin by putting worship on.

- **Honour** also ushers in the presence of God – you can begin by honouring the Holy Spirit, Jesus and His sacrifice and the Father and His love for you. Out loud, or in the silence of your heart, begin to honour the Lord.

- **Thanksgiving** – as you honour the Lord become thankful for all that He has done for you; remember times that He has been there for you and previously encountered you. Set your heart in an attitude of gratitude, as thanksgiving will lead into praise.

- **Praise** – as you are meditating on all the things the Lord has done for you, begin to turn your attention to who the Lord IS and start praising Him for His nature: that He is your provider, your healer, He is peace, love, gracious, kind, etc. move your heart into a position of praise and adoration for the king.

- **Worship** – worship is a response of your heart to God's heart. Thanksgiving draws your attention to Him, then you move into praise which is who He is. This brings you closer to Him and when you see Him, your heart responds in worship. As you respond, He is exalted and you enter into glory. Worship positions you for encounter.

- As you are worshiping you will move into the glory, the **manifest presence of God**, the all sufficiency as Abraham knew God. In the glory, God will move on your heart, and as He does, follow His leading and do, or say whatever He does and says. This is a place that is limitless, anything is possible and in this place you will encounter the Lord.

When a distraction comes, recognise it and focus back on Jesus and reconnect, continue to do this until it becomes natural. To begin with you may wish to write down all the distractions that come in to your mind. Most likely it will be things that you haven't done or still have to do. While you're starting out, just have a pad and pen next to you and create a to do list that you can complete after you finish spending time with the Lord. Hopefully this will get the distractions out of your head and allow you to refocus back on the Lord. I shut my eyes and I see my spirit pressing into the glory and I usually find myself in front of Jesus, then I ask Him to encounter me and spend time with me and give Him permission to take me or do whatever He wants to do. Then I give Him my mind, my heart and just sit in silence and wait for Him. Sometime He wants to go for a walk, other times I see myself flying to different places, or sometimes He just wants to sit and have a chat. Just spend time doing whatever He wants to do. This all takes place in my imagination. I dedicate my mind and my imagination to the Lord and allow Him access to use it to encounter Him. It's totally fine in this place to fall asleep because He may wish to encounter you with His peace. Sometimes when you fall asleep it gives Him the ability to place instructions within you. A minute asleep in God's presence is better than an hour of normal sleep. During this time with the Lord, you may feel His peace, joy or fire etc. Every time you spend time with the Lord it is different, just make note of what He is doing each day.

Take a passage of scripture such as Revelation 1:12-16 and read it over and over a number of times until it's in your mind. Then begin to meditate on the scripture by imagining the scripture. What would it look like, sound like? Imagine yourself in John's position and what he was seeing, hearing etc. Continue to imagine this and meditate on the scripture going over it in your mind. This is a tool to lead you into encounter with God. As you develop your secret place and position yourself for encounter make sure that you don't get stuck in a routine or structure. Structure is not necessarily bad, but if you are so tied to your structure that you won't change it if God wants to, then there is a problem. For a while I had a set structure, I would wake up and read the Bible, then pray in tongues and then pray in English. One morning I went to the read the Bible and God said I want you to pray in tongues first. So I began praying in tongues. An hour later I went to read the Bible and He said keep praying in tongues, so I kept praying. He began bringing scriptures to my mind to focus and meditate on while praying in tongues, but I didn't make it to the physical Bible for a few days. Why? He was trying to get me out of religion into relationship. Don't go to God with a plan of what you will do, begin hanging out with Him and asking what He wants to do. There's nothing wrong with having discipline and structure, as long as you are in relationship and happy to change what you have planned, if God is doing something else. Honestly you really want to be doing what God is doing, Bill Johnson says "if you read the Bible and don't have an encounter you have just become more religious". If we are doing the same thing every day, when God is actually wanting to meet us somewhere else, then we are really just becoming more religious: it's all about relationship. Relationship is the purpose of the secret place, therefore, everything you do while in the secret place must be done for this purpose. Ask the Father what He wants to do today, should you read the word first, pray in tongues or just sit at His feet.

Visions revealing the Kingdom

I've talked about how to encounter the Lord, and I want to briefly describe some of the encounters that I have had with the Lord, and what I learnt through them. My hope is that I may show you that these are normal, and encourage you to open yourselves up to God speaking to you through many different avenues. You see every encounter should lead you deeper into relationship with Jesus; that is the purpose of an encounter to receive a greater revelation in some way, of Him. Personally, in my own life, God has used visions or pictures in my imagination to help me understand my power and authority, and to teach me many things about the kingdom. We need to position ourselves before the Lord and give Him time to encounter us and talk to us about who we are, and the authority and power He has given us.

I thought I would share just a couple of different pictures that God gave me, to demonstrate how God can show us these things through visions or encounters. I hope that these visions will also help you to be able to see the revelation that was shown to me through them. It is important to always make sure that your encounters line up with the word of God: if something is contrary to the word then throw it away and just keep the things that line up. As you read these encounters that I have had, you have the ability to enter into these encounters and experience them yourself. This is the same with the Bible. As you are reading a story, begin meditating on the word and begin imagining the scene playing out in your mind, and you can actually enter into the scriptures and encounter the Holy Spirit through them. Allow the Holy Spirit to encounter you while you read the word and also as you read these following encounters.

I saw a vision of me walking into a cloud of glory with a staff, and I walked out of the cloud as a lion covered in the glowing presence of His glory. The staff symbolizes authority and power, (think of Moses) when I left the cloud I moved with the power and authority in me and through me, not from an external source. I walked into the cloud with fear and insecurity as a man, weak. When I came out I was fearless, I walked with confidence, boldness, head high, a king with the authority of the kingdom of heaven. My insecurity was gone and I walked with absolute power. Every sound that left my mouth put terror into demons, and I sought them out and killed them. This is the transforming power of the glory of God. In this encounter He was showing me the importance of spending time in His glory and the authority and power that comes from spending time with Him.

I was lying on the ground and the Holy Spirit hit me and I began to laugh, while I was laughing I started having all these visions. I could see cancers with smiley faces all over them and I was just laughing hysterically at them and Holy Spirit was telling me "God is so much bigger, it's like the devil is an ant and God is a giant and you are in Christ." He told me that cancer had gotten too much of a reputation in my life and I had made it too big in my life, and God wanted to resize my thinking on cancer. Well He sure did that. My hands felt so electrified it was crazy, and then Holy Spirit said, "your hands are loaded." Then I shot this huge fireball of Him at the cancer and it was destroyed. He said that I have enormous power in my hands, and I can release it into people, even when I don't have the feeling of the power, to remember that it's always there and I have access to use it. Then I saw myself walking down the street as a bonfire and I saw many people, who didn't know God, walking as pieces of wood, and fire started jumping off me and consuming the wood and turning them into mini bonfires.

This forever changed the way I see sickness and disease. I always knew how much bigger God is, but He was also showing me the power that I carried and giving me a glimpse of my calling and what I was going to do.

I saw a dragon flying around, breathing fireballs at me, then I saw an angel catch the fireballs and whirl them away. Then I saw a dragon again breathing fire on me and a bunch of angels all lying around me like a shield, and they were just sun baking in the fire as if it wasn't hurting them at all, and it wasn't getting anywhere near me. Then I saw me walking through hundreds of thousands of demons that were trying to attack me, but I'm just walking in perfect rest, with legions of angels surrounding me with baseball bats enjoying themselves while hitting all the demons away.

God was showing me the power of the angels around me and how they protect me in this war. He was taking away all stress and worry from my life and allowing me to rest in the midst of war.

He showed me what sort of life we should have and what relationship He created us to be in with Him. In the Garden of Eden He had a perfect relationship, a friendship with Adam and Eve, He walked with them daily, chatting. He hung out with them all the time in the garden. He loved them, and they loved Him and there was no sickness or disease, no pain or suffering. This is the relationship that He created us to have, and because of the wondrous act on the cross, Jesus has put us into an even better relationship than we had available before the cross. We are now above angels, seated in heavenly places with an inheritance as a son of God and co-heir with Christ. God wants to have that perfect relationship that He created us for, He doesn't want any sickness or disease, no injury, pain or suffering in our lives, therefore I should never doubt whether God wants someone to be healed no matter the circumstance.

He also reveals His nature and His will to us through visions.

I saw a seal swimming through water. A seal in water can catch prey and move powerfully and effectively, however on land seals are very slow, they are dependent on water. The Holy Spirit is the water, the prey represents demons. When we stay immersed in the Holy Spirit then we move powerfully, effectively and efficiently, and we are able to catch and destroy the devil; if we leave the Holy Spirit we end up on dry land and can hardly move, we can't catch prey and we die.

He gave me this illustration of the importance of staying immersed in my relationship with the Holy Spirit and how dependent I am on Him to move through me, to win the victory. God gives me visions to help me to understand the scriptures. He puts them in language that I would understand and helps me to connect. He shows me many things about all aspects of the kingdom in my time with Him through visions. These all take place in my imagination as I yield to the Holy Spirit.

Take some time now to spend with the Holy Spirit and ask Him to encounter you, and experience His presence. Ask Him to show you the power and authority that you carry in a unique way.

Your Heart is Key

In 2016 I had an intense season, partly because I was engaged, and God was preparing my heart for marriage, and the other part because He was shaping my character to be able to walk in His calling. You see God's anointing may take you places, it may open doors for you, however, it's your character that will maintain you and keep you. Your anointing can actually crush you if your character is not to a level that can carry it. We need to surrender and allow God to work on our hearts, this then helps to establish and build our character.

During this season I had two dreams in two nights. In the first dream I had an angel appear to me, I knew that his name was "God remembers you" and that was his message. The second night I was coming out of a shop and an angel appeared to me and said "God says you are powerful, but you are only walking in a small amount of the power. The key to walking in power is the heart", then he reached into my chest and grabbed my heart, and it ignited into fire and the dream was over.

But from that day all of this emotion started welling up in me, and I felt like I was having an emotional mental breakdown. There was so much emotion and I had no idea where it was coming from. I now realise that the angel triggered a refining fire in my heart, and the emotion was all the emotion and pain that I had supressed in my heart for my whole life. It was being brought to the surface so that I could submit to God and allow Him to deal with it. To be honest I was still very resistant to change, and dealing with emotion and the healing of my heart. It took me the next couple of weeks to come into more alignment. This dream happened about a week before I went to America with Melissa.

I met up with my friend Jordan and he prophesied over me and began telling me what was happening, and what would happen; why you have to deal with your heart. He said you had to deal with your heart to walk in power, and that God was taking me into the cave of David. In the cave, God would be delivering me of all the pain, hurt, offence and emotion that I had supressed and not dealt with in my life. Not just the past and present pain, but all of the future stuff that I would have to deal with. He would be building a strength into me during this season, so that when I face what God knows I will face, I will be strong. He is building the foundation in my heart to stand on. It might be a painful season but necessary so that I could walk in the power of God that I was called to walk in.

I was still resistant when we flew to Azusa St in the USA. We went for a conference and a holiday, and I spent the entire day crying. God was bringing up, and dealing with, so much emotion. I have no idea what He was dealing with, but I know that stuff was leaving and being dealt with. We then drove to Bethel Church in Redding, California which is Bill Johnson's church, where I studied. The first night I walked in with a lot of emotion and God smacked me with His love, and I cried the whole night. God delivered me of so much stuff that I left the church an entirely different person. It felt like He wiped away everything that had built up for the last 2 years, in a moment, and changed my heart.

On Saturday we went to the healing rooms and had the opportunity to spend an hour with one of my mentors Les Coombs, he was talking about love and the heart. How he and his wife spend days together just seeking the Lord, and how love is never offended and never seeks to protect itself. You don't need to protect your heart when you are free and healthy. He was talking mainly about finding your value in God's heart. About entering His heart and allowing Him to enter yours, and finding your value and identity in Him; your security in His love for you and His acceptance of you.

During the morning we received a prophetic word about the heart journey we were on, and I was just crying for hours while everyone was talking to us as my heart began to open up and receive. On Sunday we went to church and received an amazing prophetic word that talked again about the heart journey we were on, then we hung out with a good friend Jake who was talking about his heart journey, and what God had been teaching him about healing of the heart. When we went back to church at night, I got nailed again and was crying all through worship. God was talking to me about being pleasing to Him. That He wasn't disappointed in me and angry with me, but that He was pleased with me that I was accepted and loved by Him. I had an enormous fear of what I might actually find in my heart if I opened it to Him. He completely delivered me of that fear of my heart that night, there was no more fear in His presence. All the fear was gone, only His love, safety and security remained; I could open my heart to Him. He said to me **"Jason there is nothing that you can say to me that will change the way I see you."** I saw a safe place where there was no judgement, no condemnation, no guilt, no shame, just love and safety where I could be myself, and completely open my heart and share everything with Him. I saw my heart begin to soften and a crack appeared, from the crack flowed a river of living water which contained the power of God and it began to flow into my body. The process had begun and I was now able to begin to surrender my heart to Him and go on the journey two weeks after He told me I had to.

Many of us are afraid of what we might find in our hearts if we yield it to the Lord, can I encourage you that the Lord is not afraid because he already knows what's in your heart. There is nothing that you are going to reveal to Him that will change the way He thinks about you. We focus on the bad, He focuses on how He created us. If we allow Him access to our hearts and let Him deal with anything that isn't Him, then you will find that there is glory inside your heart. There is so much that God has placed in your heart that represents Him, that the enemy is wanting to keep you from experiencing and releasing. The enemy wants to keep you afraid of your heart and instigate fear so that you will never release all the glory that God has placed inside. There is actually pure light and love inside your heart waiting to be released, if you have accepted Christ and have the Holy Spirit dwelling within you. Opening your heart can be a painful process, and a scary process, but as you spend time with the Lord and allow His love to fill you, He will create a safe place for you to release all those burdens that you no longer need to carry. Allow Him into your heart, let Him get rid of any junk that might still remain in those hidden caverns that you have been too afraid or ashamed to let Him see. He will set you free with His love and give you so much peace. There is no condemnation within Him. This is a key to walking in power, allowing God to work on your heart because then you can access the fullness of the Glory and power that He has placed within your heart.

You see, the power of God flows through your heart, the more you yield your heart to the Lord and allow Him to heal and strengthen your heart, the more you position yourself for Him to allow His power to flow through you.

Let me explain it in a way the Lord showed me. Imagine a bright torch on the ground facing up. The light is very powerful and strong. Now begin to place rubbish on top of the light until you can no longer see it. Has the brightness or power of the light changed at all? No it's just being smothered, if you begin to take one piece of rubbish off at a time the light seemingly increases, however, the light actually isn't increasing it's stayed the same the rubbish is simply reducing. I feel that this is a good picture of the power of God increasing in our lives as we yield our hearts to a process of healing. The light of Christ is just as strong inside you as it ever will be, you may see more power operating through your life in a few years. However, this isn't due to an increase in power or light within you, but rather due to the healing or removal of rubbish from your heart.

One of the major keys to this healing process, I believe, is found in the life of David, the key is worship. You see God has given you the key to your own heart and He gives you the option as to whether you will unlock it and give Him access. This is because He wants to partner with you. As you worship, you unlock your heart and allow it to fully experience the Lord. Your heart is open to connect with Him and to yield to Him, and allow Him to work on you. That is why David had such a wonderful relationship with the Lord, because he always had his heart in a position of worship.

Overcoming Offence

God has been talking to me a lot about offence and how it has been keeping people from walking in their breakthrough. He said to me, "**Step over your offence and into your destiny.**" Proverbs 19:11 says" Good sense makes one slow to anger, and it is his glory to overlook an offence."

Offence is an obstacle, it keeps you from others and it keeps you from intimacy with God.

I believe that offence is one of the largest weapons the enemy uses to bring division amongst God's people, and to keep people from intimacy with Him. God showed me a picture of what offence looks like in the body, I saw a bullet being lodged into a person's body and it landed in one of their joints. The bullet caused a restriction of movement within the body; the joint was no longer able to move freely and operate in the way it was intended too. The bullet wound made the joint stiff, limiting the person with the wound. This is what offence looks like both in the body of Christ, and for individuals. A wound limits you from operating in the fullness of what God has intended for you; it restricts your movement to freely operate in your destiny. It causes difficulties for you and makes things a lot harder than what they need to be. But there is good news – if you partner with the Lord, He can help you to dislodge the bullet, remove the cause of the wound, and then allow the body to heal and repair itself so that it can freely move again.

So many people say to me, this person or that person has offended me. I've thought about this for a long time, and begun to say, 'it's impossible for someone to offend you, offence is a choice. You have to choose to be offended."

We all have the opportunity, on a daily basis, to choose offence or choose forgiveness. We need to daily be spending time with God and giving Him permission to search our hearts and bring to the surface any offence that we have agreed with. If you have agreed with it, and chosen to be offended, then it's also just as simple to disagree with it and choose to forgive. I'm not saying go introspective and spend time trying to find garbage, I'm suggesting spending time with Jesus, submitting to Him, worshipping Him, and giving Him permission to raise things with you as you talk with Him. Let God do the searching, not you. Then through relationship, let Him reveal areas to you and how to deal with them.

Side note: many of us spend so much time trying to resist the devil, myself included. "Resist the devil and he will flee from you," we quote part of the scripture. But we are missing the key ingredient. It says "submit to God, resist the devil and He will flee". Many of us are trying to resist the devil in our own strength rather than submitting to God and allowing His grace to enable us to resist the devil. Submit to God and allow His grace to enable you to forgive those you can't forgive.

Offence is a heart issue and offence will cut you off from your breakthrough, it will cut you off from relationship. Let me give you a recent example from my life. I was in church, and a friend said something to my wife and I that we interpreted the wrong way. Without knowing it we had chosen to be offended at this person and it began to play out over the next couple of weeks. We began cutting ourselves off from the person as the offence placed division and distance between us and greatly affected our relationship. One night I was reading this chapter of my book and the Lord stopped me and said "Jason you are carrying an offence", at first I was shocked, then I realised that He was right. I had been carrying an offence against my friend for a couple of weeks. In that moment I texted my friend and asked if he was available to talk. I then called and explained the situation to my friend, that I had agreed with offence that day in church when he spoke to us. I apologised for being offended at him and allowing it to cause division between us, and then asked for his forgiveness. He forgave me, apologised for the miscommunication, and then explained what he had meant by what he said. We forgave each other and prayed together for unity to be established once again. You see, sometimes I think that we can actually agree with offence without even realising it. That's why it is so important to spend time with God on a daily basis and allow Him access to your heart. Then when you do agree with offence in your heart, God is able to reveal it to you and help you to forgive and be healed.

How do you move past offence? Recognise that you have chosen to be offended, repent of the offence, go to the person, if possible, and apologise for holding offence against them, and ask for forgiveness, then forgive the person and the blockage crumbles.

It happens with God as well. We say, "God you didn't do this or that for us," and we get offended and shut down our hearts towards Him. He never shuts down His heart to us and He will never turn His back on us: it's always us who turns away. He's standing there with arms open wide, heart full of forgiveness, waiting for us to repent and come back to Him.

You see this so clearly in the story of the prodigal son, Luke 15:11-32: the son turns away from the Father demanding his inheritance and then lives a very sinful and horrific life. He wasted all of his money, but then the scripture says he came to himself and realised his error. He repented, which simply means he changed his mind, he changed his direction and turned back towards his father. What was the father's reply? He went running towards him, with his arms wide open, to embrace and kiss his son and lavish him with gifts. This is the same with us, any time we turn away from God, He is there waiting for us to come back with love in His eyes and arms open wide.

When I am operating in my own strength it's easier to choose offence than to forgive. It's actually impossible to live a life of forgiveness and be unoffendable in our own strength, but if we submit to God, and give Him our life, then it's Him living and being and having His way through us. If we allow His love, His grace and His forgiveness to flow through our hearts then the impossible begins to be possible.

We must look at the life of Jesus: how easy would it have been for Him to choose to be offended when they were nailing Him to the cross, when they were hitting Him, spitting on Him and mocking Him? Yet He chose the higher path, He cried out, "Father forgive them for they don't know what they are doing." He forgave them and He tells us, throughout scripture, to do the same. Luke 17:3-4 "Pay attention to yourselves! If your brother sins, rebuke him, and if he repents, forgive him, and if he sins against you seven times in the day, and turns to you seven times, saying, 'I repent,' you must forgive him." Matthew 18:21-22 "Then Peter came to Jesus and asked, "Lord, how many times shall I forgive my brother or sister who sins against me? Up to seven times?" Jesus answered, "I tell you, not seven times, but seventy-seven times."

You should read this whole passage of scripture, as Jesus then goes on to speak in a parable about how we should forgive others as Christ has forgiven us.

Throughout life we have been promised persecution: people will mock us, they may even spit on us or hit us and they will say offensive things, however they can never offend our hearts, no matter how much they try, because we have the choice to live in forgiveness or to partner with offence.

This is my thought process when it comes to offence and forgiveness: if someone does something against me that is wrong, I then have a choice, offence or forgiveness. How many times this year have I said or done things that could be offensive to God? How many times has He chosen to forgive me rather than cut me off from His heart through offence? If I have been forgiven so many times by my Heavenly Father how can I not forgive the person who just hurt me, and ask God to heal me and fill me with a greater measure of His love? Let me show you the power of offence in a scripture that is very regularly misquoted.

Mark 6:2-6 "What are these remarkable miracles he is performing? Isn't this the carpenter? Isn't this Mary's son and the brother of James, Joseph, Judas and Simon? Aren't his sisters here with us?" And they took offence at him. Jesus said to them, "A prophet is not without honour except in his own town, among his relatives and in his own home." He could not do any miracles there, except lay his hands on a few sick people and heal them. He was amazed at their lack of faith."

Many people misquote this scripture and say that Jesus couldn't do any miracles. The fact is we don't know what miracles He couldn't do there but we do know that He could heal the sick because it says that "he laid his hands on a few sick people and healed them." I believe the key to understanding this scripture is actually in verse 3 where it says "they took offence at Him." I believe it was their offence that caused the unbelief that kept them from bringing the sick to Jesus. It was also offence in the Pharisees' hearts that kept them from seeing Jesus for who He really was.

For example: imagine you were offended. Then you went through a struggle in your life and it was the person by whom you were offended, who carried the answer to your problem. Wouldn't your offence keep you from approaching that person? This is what I believe happened, they didn't honour Jesus, they were offended by Him, and **it was this offence that kept them from coming to Jesus**, and it kept them from bringing the sick to Him. You cannot tell me that if someone sick was brought or came out to Jesus that He wouldn't have healed them. No, everyone who came to Jesus, without exception, was healed.

You see, offence works the same way in our life, whether it is our spouse, our friends, a random person or God Himself. We need to ask God to search our hearts and give us the grace to forgive and release that offence to Him, to heal our hearts and open them back up, so that we can move forward.

Offence will keep you locked into the problems of the past. Forgiveness will propel you into the future.

One last thing I'd like to mention: one reason it feels so difficult to forgive and feels easier to stay offended, is because the root of our offence is actually pride. I thought about this the other day. Why would I still be offended at someone? I thought "well because they did the wrong thing towards me, I deserve to feel the way I do because of the way they treated me." We will find so much freedom if we just gave up our rights to feel offended and hurt. Die to yourself, give up your rights, give up your life into God's hands and walk into freedom. This is a process of humility. It takes humility to forgive someone, and humility destroys pride. The Bible says, "pride comes before a fall but the humble are exalted." Every area of your life in which you have agreed with offence, there is an opportunity for breakthrough and freedom today. Turn your obstacle of offence today, into your instrument for breakthrough.

So practically here are some steps.

> 1. Take some time to ask the Lord to reveal any offence in your hearts.
> 2. Ask Him how much He has forgiven you and how much He loves you.
> 3. Ask Him how He sees that person with whom you are offended and how much He loves them.
> 4. Ask for the grace to release the offence and forgive.
> 5. Then simply give it to God, forgive and release the offence. The reason that this will only work through grace and relationship, is because it's not a head thing: you have to submit your heart to the Lord and release the offence from your heart.

I believe that if you spend time getting the Word into you, then you begin to interact with the word in your time with the Lord. The Holy Spirit takes the word that you have been reading and reveals it to you when you spend time with Him.

Walking a Life of Power

As seen in the previous chapters, Identity and Intimacy are the foundation from which the power of God flows. Now that we have established the foundation, it's time to discuss why the power of God needs to operate in our lives, and then some practical tips on how to operate in that power.

Why should we walk in the power of God?

1 Corinthians 2:4-5 "My message and my preaching were not with wise and persuasive words, but with a demonstration of the Spirit's power, so that your faith might not rest on human wisdom, but on God's power."

1 Corinthians 4:20 "For the kingdom of God is not a matter of talk but of power."

Matthew 10:7-8 "As you go, proclaim this message: 'The kingdom of heaven has come near.' Heal the sick, raise the dead, cleanse those who have leprosy, drive out demons. Freely you have received; freely give."

Luke 10:9 Heal the sick who are there and tell them, 'The kingdom of God is near you.'

We should walk in the power of God because it is how Jesus taught His disciples to share the gospel. Everywhere Jesus went He was proclaiming, "the kingdom of heaven is near" and then He would demonstrate the power and dominion of the kingdom. Jesus was showing us how our lives should look. Everywhere you go the Kingdom of Heaven goes, so you can announce the Kingdom of Heaven has come near and then demonstrate it. This was Jesus' evangelism model.

The Power of God must be seen

I was spending time with the Lord one day when He began to speak to me about Philip and how he transformed a nation in a couple of days. This is a model that I think needs to be replicated and released in our day and age. Can a nation be saved in a day? I believe the answer is yes.

Acts 8:5-13 "5 Philip went down to a city in Samaria and proclaimed the Messiah there. 6 When the crowds heard Philip **and saw the signs he performed, they all paid close attention to what he said.** 7 For with shrieks, impure spirits came out of many, and many who were paralysed or lame were healed. 8 So there was great joy in that city. 9 Now for some time a man named Simon had practiced sorcery in the city and amazed all the people of Samaria. He boasted that he was someone great, 10 and all the people, both high and low, gave him their attention and exclaimed, "This man is rightly called the Great Power of God." 11 They followed him because he had amazed them for a long time with his sorcery. 12 But when they believed Philip as he proclaimed the good news of the kingdom of God and the name of Jesus Christ, they were baptized, both men and women. 13 Simon himself believed and was baptized. And he followed Philip everywhere, astonished by the great signs and miracles he saw."

Philip proclaimed the Messiah, Jesus is Lord. Why did they pay close attention to what he said? Because of the signs he was performing. What were these signs? Demons were cast out and the sick were healed.

Do you want to bring great joy to your area and your city? Here is how you can do it. Miracles, signs and wonders will bring great joy to your city.

There was a well-known sorcerer in the city who had amazed the people with his power for some time, they called him the Great Power. Does this sound like our day? Haven't the psychics, the mediums and all the demonic sorcerers been coming out of hiding, and are now on full display in this city? I walked along the esplanade with my friend a while back and there was a lady with a tent, unashamedly charging people for healing and psychic readings. Why do people go to psychics, mediums, raeke or any other demonic kind of healing? Because we, as a body, are not demonstrating the full power of God.

Let's continue in the story. When the city saw the power that Philip operated in they believed in Jesus and were baptised. Even Simon the great demonic power of that day, who had been amazing them with his power for a long time, believed and was baptised when he saw the true power of God. You see Simon knew the power he walked in, and he knew that his power was nothing in comparison to a son of God operating in true power. It wasn't until the city saw a believer operating in the full power of God that they repented and gave their lives to God, even the satanist of the area.

But this is my favourite line in the entire story. "And he followed Philip everywhere, *astonished* by the great signs and miracles he saw." Why is the world not saying that about Christians today? The world should be astonished by the great signs and miracles that they see through our lives. It's when we start walking in our identities and start operating in the fullness of the power of God out there for the world to see, that's when the power of the demonic will be shown for what it really is: fake and weak in comparison to God. When we start operating in the power of God, our city will come to Christ, the satanists will come flocking to the church and there will be great joy in the city. Why are satanists still operating in our city, why are the psychics and raeke healers still operating? Because they aren't yet astonished by the power we are walking in.

Here's another story I love which demonstrates the same point. Acts 5:12-16 "The apostles performed many signs and wonders among the people. And all the believers used to meet together in Solomon's Colonnade. No one else dared join them, even though they were highly regarded by the people. Nevertheless, more and more men and women believed in the Lord and were added to their number. As a result, people brought the sick into the streets and laid them on beds and mats so that at least Peter's shadow might fall on some of them as he passed by. Crowds gathered also from the towns around Jerusalem, bringing their sick and those tormented by impure spirits, and all of them were healed."

How were people being saved? The apostles were performing many signs and wonders to the extent that there was regional revival, and people started coming from far away bringing their sick and laying them in the street. Why are people not lining the streets with the sick for us to walk past, and why are they not lining up outside the churches? Because we are not walking in the fullness of the power of God that is available to us. Now please hear me, I am not putting condemnation on anyone, what I want to do is show you what is possible, what is available, and make you hungry to seek the Lord. How many people were healed in this passage of scripture? *All.*

The power of God must be demonstrated with the preaching of the gospel, if you want your neighbourhood, city or nation to encounter God, be saved and transformed. The power of God shows that He is real, He is alive and He is loving people today. It demonstrates God's heart and represents Him to the world.

I don't believe we are waiting for God to pour out His spirit upon us, I think He has already done everything He is going to do, and He is now waiting for us to realise who we are, stand up, and make our difference in history. If we start stepping out, I believe we are about to see some of the most incredible miracles that have ever occurred in history, and I want you to begin dreaming with God.

I spend hours dreaming with God about my city…having a line of ambulances outside the front door for us to pray for, having a 24/7 prayer station at the church because ambulances will drive by the church before going to hospital with their patients. Having a place at the hospital for people to see us before they see the doctors, entire hospitals being cleared out. Destroying sickness and disease in the entire city, then what do we do when there is no more sickness or disease? What do we do with the hospitals, what do we do with the staff? Train them to heal the sick.

What about a sickness free zone in your city? When people drive into the area they get healed, or as they enter your church they are instantly healed. What about when tourists and visitors drive across the border or land in your airport and they instantly get healed?

What is possible with God?

You may think I'm crazy, however, many of these dreams I have, have already taken place in our history:

Most of Wales was saved in a couple of years in the Welsh revival, all the bars and police stations were closed down because there was no crime.

At Azusa Street in California U.S.A., the presence was so thick that people were healed and slain by the Spirit a number of blocks away, getting off the train, and it was recorded in the newspaper.

"The Voice of healing" revival, in U.S.A. during the 50's, had mile long lines of people coming to be healed.

John G Lake conservatively recorded 9 out of 10 people being healed when he ministered in the great revival in South Africa.

This has already happened in our lifetime, so of course it can happen again.

Power of the Holy Spirit

It's important to remember that you are completely reliant on the Holy Spirit because He is the operator of the power.

In Acts 1:8 Jesus is speaking to His disciples and He says "But you will receive power when the Holy Spirit comes on you; and you will be my witnesses in Jerusalem, and in all Judea and Samaria, and to the ends of the earth."

So, we see here a couple of reasons the Holy Spirit was sent, and what He does. The first thing is that you will receive power when the Holy Spirit comes on you. The purpose of this power is to be a witness to the ends of the earth, to enable you to share the gospel of Jesus Christ with people you meet, and to become His witness. The Holy Spirit equips you with courage and boldness to share the gospel.

In Acts 2 the Holy Spirit falls on Peter and the other disciples and what happens? This man who just denied Jesus and was hiding from the Jews with the other disciples, now is standing in front of 3,000 people declaring the word of God with boldness, declaring that Jesus is Lord, and telling them to repent. He's speaking to the same people who just a few days earlier killed Jesus. He said the Holy Spirit made them drunk and they lost all of their fear and became bold and courageous.

The power of the Holy Spirit is also to enable you to do the same healing and miracles that Jesus did, to continue showing the world that God is real and that He loves them and demonstrating that the kingdom of God is near, by healing the sick, raising the dead and casting out demons. We see this in Acts 10:38 "how God anointed Jesus of Nazareth with the Holy Spirit and power, and who went about doing good and healing all who were under the power of the devil, because God was with him."

The Holy Spirit empowered Jesus to heal the sick and deliver the oppressed. He was given to us to continue doing the same works. John 14:12 "I tell you the truth anyone who believes in me will do the same things that I have been doing and even greater things than these because I go to the father and I will do whatever you ask in my name."

Jesus said we would do the same miracles and greater because when He left, the Holy Spirit was sent to us.

What are some other reasons the Holy Spirit was sent? To teach us all things, be our counsellor and our comforter. John 14:26 "But the Advocate, the Holy Spirit, whom the Father will send in my name, will teach you all things and will remind you of everything I have said to you." Just like the disciples had Jesus to do relationship with, and to teach them all things from the Father, we now have the Holy Spirit with whom we grow in relationship, and He will teach us all things.

He will be there for us when we need Him to give us counsel with regard to different situations, when we need comfort in hard times, or times of persecution, and to teach us by revealing the scriptures and taking us into a deeper intimacy with the Father.

The Holy Spirit also intercedes for you, He prays the perfect will of God over your life, when you don't know what to pray; submit to Him and allow Him to pray on your behalf. He will build you up, strengthen you and encourage you. Romans 8:26 "In the same way, the Spirit helps us in our weakness. We do not know what we ought to pray for, but the Spirit himself intercedes for us through wordless groans."

He also testifies to your spirit that you are a child of God, and He reminds you that you are the righteousness of Christ. He helps to guide you and keep you on the path of righteousness. Romans 8:16 "The Spirit himself testifies with our spirit that we are God's children."

We need to spend time cultivating our relationship with the Holy Spirit as He seriously is the most important person with whom you can ever spend time, and He was sent to be your helper on the earth. However, always remember that the Holy Spirit is a person and He is God. We need to worship the Holy Spirit and have the same fear, reverence and respect for Him that we have for Jesus and the Father.

Accessing the Power of God through Love

We know that all the power of God flows through the Holy Spirit, but He has chosen to partner with us to release His power to people. God showed me that one way to partner with Him to release His power, was through love. He said "The secret to your ministry will be love. My power will flow through your love for me and your love for my people."

Ever since this revelation, each time before I minister to anyone, I ask God how much He loves the person that is standing in front of me. This allows me to access His heart for them, and see them through His eyes. It instantly shifts me into a perspective of seeing from a heavenly abundant perspective. It's His love through me for the people that will access His power to set them free. I don't have much to do in the equation except ask the question, receive and release the answer. This is backed up by many scriptures, it says in 10 different stories that Jesus was moved with compassion and healed the sick, or raised the dead or multiplied the food. Jesus was operating through compassion that released the power for the miracles.

Love is the foundation for absolutely everything in life, everything flows from love. God is love and we were created in his image, we were created in the image of love. **The natural by-product of finding out our identity and the nature of our Father, is us becoming love** and then walking out what love actually looks like. I woke up the other day with this thought in mind, we are the dwelling place of the presence of God and He is love. This means we are full of the love of God. Then I found an amazing scripture in Romans 5:5 which says "God's love *has* been poured out into our hearts through the Holy Spirit, who has been given to us." How about we meditate on the love that He *has* already poured into our hearts, and release this to the world before asking for more. As we give away His love, He will constantly pour more into our hearts through the Holy Spirit. Look at the fruit of the spirit, all of them are founded in love which is the first one mentioned. If you love someone you will operate in all the fruit of the spirit. Galatians 5:22-23 "But the fruit of the Spirit is love, joy, peace, forbearance, kindness, goodness, faithfulness, gentleness and self-control. Against such things there is no law." You don't need to try and walk in all the fruit of the spirit, because if you just focus on becoming love, then you will automatically walk in them all.

If you want to operate more in the supernatural then spend more time understanding the love of God for yourself first, and then for everyone you meet. Jesus says in John 13:34-35 "A new command I give you: Love one another. As I have loved you, so you must love one another. By this everyone will know that you are my disciples, **if you love one another.**" Jesus says that *love* is the sign that you are one of his disciples.

Ephesians 3:17-19 "I pray that you, being rooted and established in love, may have power, together with all the Lord's holy people, to grasp how wide and long and high and deep is the love of Christ, and to know this love that surpasses knowledge—that you may be filled to the measure of all the fullness of God." Paul spends an enormous amount of time telling us about how important it is to both understand and operate in love. Would you like to be filled to the measure of all the fullness of God? Paul right here says that this filling comes from knowing (experiencing) God's love, and grasping how deep His love is for us. Spend more time experiencing His love and studying what it looks like to live a life of love.

1 Corinthians 13:4-8 is a famous passage however, we shouldn't become too familiar with it, take some time to meditate on this scripture and begin to understand who love actually is. Love does not have characteristics, love is a person. As you read this list replace love with your Father from whom all of these things are birthed, this is who He is. As we find out more about love we are finding out more about the nature of our Father, and also our identity as sons and daughters. "Love is patient, love is kind. It does not envy, it does not boast, it is not proud. It does not dishonour others, it is not self-seeking, it is not easily angered, it keeps no record of wrongs. Love does not delight in evil but rejoices with the truth. It always protects, always trusts, always hopes, always perseveres. Love never fails."

In the previous verses in this chapter it talks about different things, however without love they are all worthless. Verse 2 says "if I have a faith that can move mountains, but do not have love, I am nothing." You see, if you operate in the giftings of the Holy Spirit and you heal the sick, raise the dead, cast out demons, but do these things without understanding the love of God, without operating out of His love and extending His love to the people you are ministering to, then you may as well stop right now because power without love can be damaging and dangerous. Loving people is more important to God than anything else it is his number one priority, out of love flows everything.

God showed me that I do not have the power in my human strength to love every person who stands before me, people who persecute me and ridicule me. I struggle to love them and I realised that I struggle to love them because of one word – 'I'. However, He showed me that each time this struggle comes across my path, if I learn to surrender and yield to the Holy Spirit, then I can allow the love of God to flow through me and release His love to the person who is in front of me. I don't need to be able to love everyone in my own strength, because I have access to the love of Christ and if I will yield He will love people through me. This level of compassion requires a very open heart and can therefore create large disappointments and pain as well. Hence, in the next chapter I will be discussing some of these moments and how I have learnt to deal with them.

Perseverance and Overcoming Disappointments

This is a chapter that I wish I didn't need to write. People don't want to talk about this, however, I would rather you be prepared and equipped than pretend it doesn't exist. My mentor Chris Gore who is the Director of Healing Ministries at Bethel Church says "how you handle the disappointments of today will determine the fruitfulness of what you walk in tomorrow." Our standard for ministry is Jesus Christ and He saw every single person who came to Him healed without exception. You should never lower this standard in your life no matter what happens. For reasons that no one can yet explain we go on a journey of closing the gap between where we are at, and actually living in the standard of Jesus. Bill Johnson puts it this way, "there is a difference between what you have in the bank and what you have in your possession. Our job is to work out how to get what is in the bank into our hands."

I pray that we have progressive revelation in this area to teach people in the future, so they don't need to go through this process. From the gospels we can see that imperfect men were given the power and authority of Jesus, and they went about healing all sorts of diseases and casting out demons, and this was before they were baptised in the Spirit. They were still in the old covenant. We are only told one story about some of the disciples who were not able to set one man free, however it would seem that they operated in the same miracles and power as Jesus did. The same can be seen in the book of Acts; once they were baptised in the Holy Spirit they began operating in the same measure as Jesus had. I believe God wants to do this again, and I pray that He shows someone what we are missing. Until then however, I will share my journey with how I have had to overcome people not being healed, people dying, and the constant disappointments of the healing ministry.

This is the main reason that not many people are going after praying for the sick, because this ministry carries a huge price tag emotionally. If people are simply interested in operating in power then they will give up quickly, because they will find you actually enter into the people's pain, you enter the heart of God and your heart breaks for the sick. You will hear people who operate in the miraculous constantly sharing testimonies of people they have seen Jesus heal through them, and people think that it's all fun and games. However, not many people know the other side of the story. People don't know the pain, the heart ache and the hours of tears they have sown on the floors of their bedrooms, to see what they see.

Compassion comes with an emotional price tag. You see, when you become close to the heart of God, you feel what He feels, your heart begins to break for what His breaks for. He allows you to experience brief glimpses of His compassion for the sick, because if He allowed you to experience it all, it would kill you. You get to celebrate many, many victories of people being healed, even people who have been on their death beds, and trust me, when you see one of these victories it is worth your entire life praying for the sick. However, there is still pain when you lose a battle that you know you should win, losses in fact are amplified when you know the price Jesus has paid for them to be healed. It is important for you to never became calloused to the pain of losing a battle, but instead use this pain to strengthen you in the fight. I have prayed for many people who haven't been healed in the last 6 years, I'm telling you it should still bother you when someone doesn't get healed because you know the price Jesus paid and you know the love He has for that individual.

I will share just a couple of stories with you because I don't want to focus on the negatives for too long. I still remember the faces of many of the people who have not been healed, however the pain and the burden from these people have now been lifted which I'll explain later.

The first mission trip I ever went on was to South Africa in my first year at Bethel. We went to a HIV support centre and prayed for many sick people. The majority of them were instantly healed or dramatically improved including a blind woman I prayed for, however we went to one house in particular. It was a tiny little house and I will never forget this as long as I live. We walked inside the house and the family was standing around waiting for us, on the ground lying under a sheet was a twisted mess of a person. You couldn't tell if it was a boy or a girl, the body was more contorted then anyone I have ever seen, he was 18 years old and had never spoken a word in his life and had never moved in his life. His entire existence had been stuck in this torture chamber of a body unable to move or speak. He was in constant pain because all his muscles were seized, and he had arthritis in every joint. To move was agony, so he spent his whole life just lying on the ground. We began praying for this boy excited for his healing. After a few minutes nothing had happened and the questions started coming. We lay down next to him and hugged him, released the Father's love on him, we tried to cast out demons, we released love, we bound, we loosed and nothing changed in the 45 minutes that we were praying for this boy, with his family watching the entire thing. I left that place more broken hearted than I had ever been in my life, with more questions than I'd ever had, with more anger at the enemy than ever before.

So what did I do? I spent time alone with my Father and I cried, I broke down in His presence and cried my heart out to Him. I gave Him the burden of that boy and asked Him to release more power for the next one I came across. I knew it was not His fault. If Jesus was standing there the boy would have been healed. I just prayed for strength to keep my eyes on Him next time I was in a situation like that, for more power to see the next one delivered.

I was in Mexico doing a house meeting and there were around 30 people in the room and I began praying for people. They all waited their turn and 29 out of 30 people were healed. However, I can recall the face of the little girl who wasn't, she was beautiful maybe 8 or 9 years old, she was totally deaf and mute from birth, and her parents brought her to the meeting to be healed. I prayed for her at the very beginning around 6 or 7 times and absolutely nothing happened, so I said I'd pray for others and come back to her. The parents waited patiently and I prayed for the next person, a little boy who had flat feet and everyone watched as his arches grew back, I went and placed my hands on this girl's ears, nothing. I prayed for the next girl who was healed of lupus, prayed for the little girl, nothing, everyone in the room was healed except this little girl I prayed for probably in excess of 15 times that morning.

The same thing happened again in Mexico, a lady deaf mute from birth started manifesting demons that were trying to kill her, by choking her to death. Her husband next to her was also deaf mute from birth. My friend was praying for him and his ears opened and he began to speak for the first time in his life. We all prayed for his wife, nothing happened, we prayed for probably 30 or more minutes and she was in the same place when she left deaf, mute and demon possessed, but her husband was hearing and speaking. That's enough of those stories but what do you do in these situations?

Well I can only tell you what I do. At the end of each day I go back to my room and I give thanks to God for all the miracles I have seen. I give Him all the glory for the miracles I have been privileged to be used in, and then I lay down all the burdens of the people who have not been healed, and I place them in His hands, then I get on my face and ask Him for a greater revelation of who He is in me and through me. On those particular days which are extremely hard, I do the same thing. I go to my room I give Him the glory and then I give Him the burdens and I generally cry for hours until He takes it from me. Then He refills me with His love, compassion, comfort and strength to take on the next day. I can't stress how important it is to give these burdens over to God. I know from personal experience what happens if you don't, you have a mental breakdown, you get emotional and you start crying for absolutely no reason, just balling your eyes out and you are wondering why. It's because you are carrying too many burdens that don't belong to you. Spend some time with the Father and give them to Him. You may be able to handle one burden of a person not being healed, but try praying for 10, 20 or 50 people a week who aren't healed and see if you can bear up under the weight. We need to constantly be going back to the Father and being refreshed and refilled with His love.

I believe that everyone will walk through this differently in life, and so just remain sensitive to the Holy Spirit's leading. He is our comforter and our guide and He will lead you through the process. You will, at some point in your journey, come to the point where you have a decision to make, whether you give up and never pray for another person again, or decide to never give up and look forward to the next person to pray for. This is the crucial decision, and I have been at that point a few times in my life. I'm going to let you read a couple of my journey entries during these times in my life, because I hope it will give you insight and help you during the same period that you will go through. You will be able to see my progression from one year to the next, how I learned not to blame God and I learned an important key.

19th October 2011

I had a horrible start to the day today, I've been praying for Bec's friend's baby who was born almost dead and they said there was no chance, she died today. I was incredibly angry at the devil but honestly also at God because I'd prayed and He hadn't saved the baby. I know it's not his will for the baby to die, I know it's his will for the baby to be healed but then why? I will never know. All I know is that God is always good. This kept me bound for the first 3 or so hours of the day, I went to revival group and we had some time to soak. I was lying on the floor thinking through everything and God said 'Jason I want to show you my heart for Ava the baby', I said no God I'm in the middle of the floor but he kept persisting. So I got up grabbed some tissues and situated myself in a chair. Then he revealed his heart to me and mine broke, I was weeping for probably 30 or more minutes. I told God honestly what I was thinking and we made up but I was still feeling pretty bad. Then we went into one of the best worship sessions I've ever been in. We started off with a fire tunnel and people were

Perseverance and Overcoming Disappointments

getting blasted and then we had a massive praise session, we did a congo line around the entire room and just danced our hearts out, I spent some time just giving absolutely everything to God and then praised him and he was faithful and we were good.

7 Nov 2012

Began with worship, then some reading, then I got news that Abigail had died and so I began worshipping again, Joel came over and we chatted about God for a while and then watched some YouTube videos of some miracles until church, then we went to the pre service prayer for a bit and during worship I broke down and had a cry, I haven't blamed God for what has happened and I never will because I know his heart breaks for what has happened, I don't know why she wasn't healed, but I know that it has fuelled the fire in my bones to go deeper with God than I ever have before to stop this from ever happening again, all I could do was praise Jesus and worship him for being good and faithful. All I could say during worship was 'I cannot be defeated, I will never quit, I will never give up, I will win'.

10 Nov 2012

Had a bad night, a lady I prayed for Kathy died in the hospital after a brain tumour killed her and then I prayed for a guy he was in a wheelchair for 23 years he wanted prayer to get out and I prayed and didn't see anything happen, I came home and cried on the floor for half an hour and then spent over an hour in the word.

This was one of those times in my life when I was praying for people and they were dying or not being healed, and I had to make a decision whether I was going to continue. It was these times, and those decisions, that made me stronger.

I made the decision that no matter what happens in my life I will never quit, I will never give up, I will never stop praying for the sick. If I give up then the devil wins. You need to come to this decision yourself, and it takes walking through some hard yards with God. You need to go to Him and spend time with Him, be free to share your feelings and emotions and allow Him to comfort you and speak to you. You can see in each of my journal entries that the key I have found to enduring these times is to remind myself how good God is, His kindness, and to make a sacrifice of praise and worship to Him, and it is a sacrifice because it isn't what you feel like doing at the time.

The other huge key to constantly moving forward past these disappointments is to constantly keep your thoughts on what God has done and what He is doing, not on what He hasn't done. Write down all the testimonies that you have seen God do in your life and meditate on them, remind yourself of these testimonies.

Fact vs Truth

I have battled with the question of what to do when you are teaching sick people the reality that Jesus paid for their healing 2000 years ago and yet it hasn't manifested in their bodies.

One day I was asking the Lord these questions and He encouraged me by taking me to a passage of scripture in Romans 4:19-21 which is talking about Abraham the father of faith and says "Without weakening in his faith, he faced the fact that his body was as good as dead—since he was about a hundred years old—and that Sarah's womb was also dead. Yet he did not waver through unbelief regarding the promise of God, but was strengthened in his faith and gave glory to God, being fully persuaded that God had power to do what he had promised."

Wow I don't know if that encourages you as much as it did me, but the father of our faith did not deny the facts in his life. He showed us that it is possible to acknowledge the facts of our situation without weakening in our faith, and to remain focused on God, and that He has the power to do what He has promised. You see there is a difference between fact and truth. The fact may be that you have cancer in your body, but the truth is that Jesus has healed you. The fact may be that you are broke financially, however the truth is that Jesus is the provider. Where are you going to allow your attention to be drawn? If you have a broken leg I'm not telling you to ignore the facts. Ignoring the facts is not faith, but being able to look at the facts while not wavering into unbelief, and believing that God has the power to heal you, is operating in faith.

Sympathy vs Compassion

Compassion: the Greek word for compassion is *splagchnizomai* which literally means *to be moved to one's bowels,* which was thought to be the seat of love and pity, hence to be moved with compassion, an expression of the deepest emotion of the day. I looked up every passage in the New Testament where this word is used. There are 10 stories, and in every case it is used just before Jesus moves in power to change their circumstances: He heals the sick, raises the dead, casts out demons, performs miracles and meets the crowds' needs with powerful teaching. I don't think it is a coincidence that every time the scriptures say Jesus is moved to compassion, immediately following is a display of the power of God over the dominion of darkness and making impossibilities bow.

How do you know when you have entered into a place of compassion rather than simply sympathy? When your thinking changes in situations, for example you see a friend in pain and instead of thinking "oh man I'm so sorry," you think, "I have the power of God to change this circumstance, man I'm so sorry, let me help you." Compassion compels action that changes circumstances, the power of God is always released through true compassion.

Also, sympathy keeps our eyes focused on the worldly view of the situation, whereas compassion moves the focus to God's view on the situation, and how He can change it through His power. It says in Luke 7:13-15 "When the Lord saw her, He felt compassion for her, and said to her, "Do not weep." And He came up and touched the coffin; and the bearers came to a halt. And He said, "Young man, I say to you, arise!" The dead man sat up and began to speak. And Jesus gave him back to his mother." Jesus saw the widow, felt compassion and then raised the dead son. Jesus saw the need, He realized that He had the power to change their circumstances and then He acted in His identity. I believe that people cannot walk in biblical compassion unless they have a knowledge of their identity and authority.

Jesus was different from all the other people in the crowd that day because He knew that He had the power to change that widow's circumstance for the glory of God. We have the same Spirit that raised Christ from the dead, we are believers in Him and we will do the same works as Christ and even greater works. We are the most powerful people on the planet, and we should be walking in compassion that compels us to action, that changes people's circumstances by releasing the power of God through us.

Let me show you two more examples from my own life of how I've seen this work. I grew up knowing God was real but not really having an intimate relationship with Him. I would see people who I knew at the shopping centre or other places with injuries and in pain, and I would sympathise with them, or at most empathise because I had experienced the same injury, however these comforting words never changed their circumstances. I lived in this place of sympathy for 20 years and never saw the power of God released into people's lives.

This is not a fun place to live. We were not born to be powerless Christians, and it was once I had a revelation of my identity that I began to understand that I actually had authority and power to change people's circumstances and not just leave them the same. This enabled me to move into a place of compassion for people, knowing that I could back it up with the power of God. This is how Jesus lived in every situation. He wouldn't leave people the same way He found them, He would be moved with compassion that compelled Him to action to change their circumstances.

An example of this was when I was at a conference a couple of years ago and I had just discovered I had access to the power of God. I was outside on the streets and I saw a person on crutches with his ankle heavily bandaged. I could see that he was in severe pain and I felt my heart go out towards him. I was moved with compassion for him because I knew that God could take away the pain. I approached the young man and asked him about his ankle; he had badly sprained it and torn some ligaments. He showed me all the pain medication in his pocket and told me how much it hurt. In the past I would have said I was sorry that he was in pain and walked away, but this time I was moved by compassion and I asked if I could pray for him. He allowed me, not thinking anything was going to happen, I prayed a short prayer and asked him to check it out. He put his foot on the ground and gasped in astonishment, his face lit up and he said, "no way, all the pain is completely gone." He gave me his crutches and started jumping up and down and running around, pain free, glorifying God.

This would not have occurred if I had not been moved by the Father's heart into a place of compassion, that compelled me into action, and released the power of God. Oral Roberts once said that it was a revelation of how much God loved

His people that began releasing more power in his meetings. He said he began to spend time with the Lord before each meeting, asking God to show him how much He loved the people to whom he was about to minister; asking to see the people through God's heart and God's eyes and it was when he began doing this that the power of God dramatically increased in his ministry. I do the same thing before meetings, not because it is some formula, but because when you spend time with God you begin to understand His heart and cry out for things that are close to His heart. I cry out to God in response to the burden and the compassion He places within me, and when I do He pours even more love for His people, and more power to change their lives. I have found that power really does flow through love.

Walking in the Prophetic

The prophetic is another operation of power that all believers should be walking in. The prophetic operates through the love and heart of God as well, and is simply hearing from God and then releasing that word to someone else. Prophecy, word of knowledge and words of wisdom all fall under the prophetic. First Corinthians 14:3 gives a definition of prophesying. "But the one who prophesies speaks to people for their strengthening, encouraging and comfort." If it is not strengthening, encouraging or comforting than don't let it come out of your mouth. It's easy to see the negative attributes of people, but the prophetic is seeing people the way God sees them, and then calling them forth into His destiny for their lives, releasing the gold in them.

In 1 Corinthians 14:25 it says "the secrets of his heart are disclosed; and so he will fall on his face and worship God, declaring that God is certainly among you." This passage is talking about prophesying in the church. If you call the gold out of a person, you tell them their dreams, their hearts desires, then they will fall to the ground worshipping God and experiencing His goodness.

When I prophesy over someone, I see them the way God sees them and then I can treat them the way God sees them, and help them to walk into their destiny.

The first step to operating in the prophetic is to realise that God wants to speak to you, He wants to share with you and He is always speaking. When you spend time with friends don't you think it would be a little strange if you did all the talking and your friend never shared anything with you? Or if you asked them a question and they didn't respond, wouldn't this be strange? When God moves on your heart with compassion for someone, then ask Him to show you how He sees them, and if there is something He wants to say to them. He is always having positive, amazing thoughts about each of us. If we ask Him to share some of those thoughts with us about ourselves or other people, then He will, and we can encourage and edify each other.

The prophetic is just another outflow of intimacy with the Father. However, it is so powerful that one word from God, released through your mouth, can drastically change someone's life. The example that helped me to understand this was of sound waves and a radio. There are always sound waves moving through the air around us, the fact that we aren't aware of them doesn't mean they don't exist. But when we realise they do exist, we can get a radio and use it to tune in to the sound waves which give us access to songs and everything else that comes through. It is the same with God. Once you realise He is always speaking, and that His thoughts are all around you like sound waves, you have the ability, through your relationship with Him, to tune in to these thoughts, through the Holy Spirit, and begin to access them.

Ways He Speaks

Once you realize that He wants to speak to you, the next step is learning to discern *how* He speaks to you. There are many different ways God can speak to you, and this is certainly not a comprehensive list, as God can do as He pleases and could create a brand new way of speaking to you. He speaks to you in a unique way for a purpose, and that purpose is relationship. The only way you can discern how He speaks is to spend time with Him. Here are a couple of ways that He could speak to you:

Pictures – this is the most common way that God speaks to me. When you ask Him to show you something, you may begin to see something in your imagination, it may be a movie, it might be a still image or a word, but you see in your imagination.

Hearing His voice – this may be the still small voice in your heart, or a loud audible voice around.

Knowing – sometimes you look at someone and you just know certain things about their life.

Feelings – you may be around someone and instantly start feeling depressed, this may be God giving you insight to help the person you are around.

Dreams – one of the most common ways God speaks is through dreams.

Scripture – He speaks through His word and actively through the Holy Spirit.

Prophesying, like all the other gifts of the Holy Spirit, and everything else in our Christian journey, takes faith and practice. Hebrews 11:6 says, "it is impossible to please God without faith. Therefore, it stands to reason that each time you step out in faith to prophesy over someone, you are pleasing God. Here's a secret: you don't know whether you are hearing God's voice, or making it up, unless you step out and take a risk. This is how you learn to discern His voice, by trying and not being afraid to fail. You can ask anyone around me, that I try to cultivate a culture of rewarding risk rather than results. If you give a word and it's completely wrong, then I'm still going to celebrate with you that you took a risk, because that is the heart of God and that is what He has shown me. He celebrates the faith it took to take the risk.

How I Grew

This is my story of growing in the prophetic. I didn't actually know what the prophetic was until I went to Bethel, even though looking back I operated in it a few times. I can remember instances at Hillsong Church when I gave people words and they held on to them as words from God. I didn't realise at the time that this was prophesy. The first week at Bethel School of Supernatural Ministry, we were put in the middle of a group and told to ask God what He had to say about someone. My first prophetic word was a scripture that I gave someone. Then Kris Vallotton began teaching us about the prophetic in school. He said that there were people in the room in whom the enemy had shut down their dream life, and God wanted to restart it. I realised I hadn't had a dream for over 10 years and so I stood, and that night I began dreaming again. During this same day Kris taught us about "The Screen", this was revolutionary to my life and really how I began to learn to prophesy. The basics are this: when you shut your eyes, there is a screen that you see in your imagination, and this is where God talks to you. When I say think of a pink elephant, you are probably seeing a pink elephant right now in your imagination. You know it is your imagination because pink elephants don't exist. This is the exact place that God uses to speak to you. Your imagination is not bad, it's simply a screen, it is what you place on the screen that determines whether it's good or bad.

I began dedicating the screen of my imagination to the Lord, and asking Him to speak to me. Then I would shut my eyes and allow Him to draw on my imagination, and believe that it was Him. This began a journey of encounters with God that transformed my life. I learned that this is the primary way that God speaks to me, and not just for myself, but I found that if I asked Him to show me the destiny of others, then He would draw a picture for me to see. As I enquired after the pictures, He would tell me what they meant, and I could release them to people.

For example, that day Kris asked us to prophesy over the person next to us. So I asked God to show me a picture for the person and I saw, in my imagination, a picture of a banana being peeled. I asked the Lord what it meant, and I said to the person "I see a banana being peeled and I believe that God is doing a work on your heart, where He is peeling back your heart to reveal what He has inside for you." That's not word for word but the general gist of what I had said. The guy confirmed that was what he felt like God was doing. This got me really excited and started me on the prophetic journey, you couldn't stop me from practicing! Who wouldn't want to be used by God? If you could be taught to hear His voice, and tell people what He is saying to them, why wouldn't you do it? Well you can learn, and I'm teaching you how. This will change your life, and more importantly it will change the lives of everyone around you, because people around you will start walking into their destinies as you prophesy over them.

At first I had to shut my eyes, be touching the person's shoulder or holding their hand, and focussing really hard to be able to pick up what God was saying. But I began practicing as we had services each Sunday night, and my friends and I would go around and prophesy over 5, 10, 15 people. Shortly I began taking my hand off the person but keeping my eyes shut so I could focus. Then I began practicing with my eyes open, and looking into the screen of my imagination while having my hand touching the person; it seemed to help me connect with them.

Your imagination is also how you see in the spirit realm. Finally I began having my eyes open and not touching them, just being able to look at them. Ultimately this is where you want to get to, because, when you are on the streets, it's a bit difficult to shut your eyes and touch someone to give them a word. I started practicing with people in school, and then I began practicing on the streets when we went out treasure hunting. Treasure hunting is where you pray before going to the streets and ask God who you are going to meet. You then write down any clothes you see, any names or ailments that He shows you. Then you go and find people who have the items on your list. Very often this leads to divine encounters with people ready for a touch from God.

Something Kris Vallotton taught us at school is that with every word God shows you, there is a process of revelation, interpretation and application. Here's an example:

My first word was about a banana, the picture of the banana was the revelation, I then asked God for the interpretation, what it means. I then needed to ask how to apply it to the person's life; was I supposed to say everything I was seeing or just part of it? Sometimes God shows you things about a person that you aren't supposed to say, but are to be used for intercession. So, you need to ask not only for the interpretation, but for how to apply that word to the person's life.

You might find times when you think your word has one interpretation, when actually it has another that will speak directly to the person. I would encourage you to just speak simply and plainly what you see. Here's an example:

I was ministering in the healing rooms at Bethel that are setup at the church on a Saturday morning. People from all over the world come, and we have a team of around 100 people to pray and minster healing to them. We were praying for a lady and I started seeing a rose in my mind. I was asking the Lord to show me something else for the lady but all I could see was the rose, and He wasn't telling me anything about the rose. Honestly I thought this was a prophetic word that I was going to release the fragrance of the rose of Sharon or something. Something else I've learnt with the Lord, is that sometimes you have to step out and say the first thing you are seeing before He will release any more to you. So I asked the lady, does a rose mean anything to you? The lady instantly burst into tears and said that her favourite Aunt Rose had just died and she was grieving over the loss. I was able to comfort her that God knew what she was going through and was there for her.

So how can you practically introduce this into your life? Begin in safe, small groups, either with friends or in your connect/home group, or just at church on a Sunday. I recommend starting out practising in church because, as you do, you will build a history with God, and people can give you feedback. As you experience more and more that you are hearing from God, it will increase your faith and confidence, and then you begin to start prophesying on the streets, over your work colleagues or in restaurants. When I was practicing the prophetic I always tried to ask for feedback. I would encourage you, especially in the beginning, to ask some questions – ask for feedback every time you prophesy. How did that make you feel? Were you encouraged? Did it resonate with you? "No" is not a bad answer as you are learning. Celebrate the risk. Lastly, don't be afraid to prophesy: this is how I think about it, **at worst you are going to encourage someone, at best you will completely transform their life**, either way is a win.

As you begin walking in the prophetic you begin to understand how incredibly powerful it really is. You have the ability to change atmospheres with your words, to change lives, to remind people who God says they are and help them to rise to His standard for their life.

If you see bad things or sin in people's lives don't say it because you have the power of life and death in your tongue, and you will agree with the negative and empower it. Speak the opposite, or firstly ask the Holy Spirit what you should be declaring over them. They don't need to know that you see the negative as it won't make them feel good. Test the prophetic word on yourself; if you wouldn't want to receive it then don't give it.

If you would like to grow in this gifting then I would suggest some activation exercises that helped me. The only way to grow in the prophetic is to begin prophesying over people.

Activation

Get some friends over and begin worshipping, then practice hearing the Lord. I always begin by thanking the Lord that I hear His voice, and thanking Him that He loves the person standing before me and that He wants to speak to this person. I ask the Lord to show me His heart and how He sees the person before me, and to use me to release a word to them. Then have fun.

Have someone stand in front of you, then ask the Lord, if this person were an animal what animal would they be? Then ask for the attributes about that animal that apply to the person. You can also ask what Bible character the Lord wants to show you for the person, then ask what aspects of the Bible character He is highlighting for this person. Or even ask the Lord what piece of furniture they might be, and then what it is about that piece of furniture that He wants to speak to the person about. These are just some questions to prompt you and get you started. Over time this isn't necessary.

The next activation: You can have one line of people with their eyes shut, then place a person in front of each of them and put the hand of the person praying onto the shoulder of the person standing in front of them, and then ask them to prophesy. This way you can't see the person with your physical eyes, and are forced to only pick up on what the Lord is saying in the spirit. Even attempt some words of knowledge about whether the person is male or female and colour of hair etc. Make sure it is a safe place to practice.

Ask questions of God, how do you see this person? Who is this person to you?

How did you create this person? What have you called them to do? What do you love about this person?

Operating in Healing and Miracles

Personally, this is my favourite operation of the power of the Holy Spirit. Jesus told us the key to operating in His power in John 5:19 "Very truly I tell you, the Son can do nothing by himself; he can do only what he sees his Father doing, because whatever the Father does the Son also does. For the Father loves the Son and shows him all he does." Why does the Father show His son all things? Because He loves Him. Knowing how much you are loved by the Father will give you the access to receive the secrets of His heart. Focus on His love for you. Intimacy with the Holy Spirit is the key to operating in the miraculous; knowing His heart for the sick, and operating out of His love and compassion for the people you meet. Being able to see what the Father is doing and hear what He is saying so that you can copy Him.

Jesus says he can do *nothing* by himself. He didn't do any of the miracles. Jesus is showing us how to live life, we need to know that we can do *nothing* without relationship with God. Jesus perfectly models how we should live, He knew that He could do nothing, and then shows us how to have a relationship with the Father and the Holy Spirit and cooperate with them for His name to be glorified. We should do the same thing, God does not *need* us to work miracles, He wants to use us. He chose to redeem us, make us His sons and allow us to work with Him to see the sick healed. Why? In John He says pray so that your joy may be full. As we cooperate with God He does all the work and we get to be filled with joy. We need to live a life of humility knowing that God has chosen us, and that it is a privilege to be used by Him; it is His words, power and love, but we get to be the vessels He flows through.

I just thought of a passage in Matthew 8:10 which says, "When Jesus heard this, He was amazed..." Have you ever wondered about this scripture, this proves that Jesus was operating on the earth as a man in relationship with the Father and Holy Spirit? Jesus did not know everything that was going to happen in His everyday life, He only knew what He saw the Father doing. This is because He had decided to not walk in His divinity, but walk purely as a man so that we could copy His life.

In the beginning, the Holy Spirit was hovering over the earth, the Father released the word (Jesus) who went forth and the Holy Spirit created. How did Jesus operate during His life? He would see what the Father was doing and hear what He was saying, then the Living Word would speak and the Holy Spirit would create or fulfil the word that was spoken. Jesus didn't do any of the miracles, it was the Holy Spirit through Him. The Holy Spirit was the power. So how should we live life? We need to see and hear what the Father is doing and saying, and release the word forth, so that the Holy Spirit can fulfil the word. You see, we are one with Christ, we are in Him, therefore when we speak they are His words not our own. Even Jesus did not speak His own words, He says in John 12:49 "For I did not speak on my own, but the Father who sent me commanded me to say all that I have spoken." Maybe more things will change in the world as believers begin opening their mouths and declaring what they see the Father doing.

How do we see what the Father is doing? There is no shortcut, it is all about building a relationship with Him. How do you grow in a relationship with your friends? You spend time with them, you ask them questions, you listen to them. This is the same with your relationship with God: spend time with Him, ask Him questions, listen to the answers and listen for questions that He will ask you, learn to understand who He is, what He does and why. Read the love letters that He has sent you in the word, learn about His nature and character from miracles that you hear about or read about in the word. You learn to recognise someone's voice by spending time with them. We learn to be more sensitive to our Father's voice as we spend time with Him and allow Him to speak to us. It is through relationship and intimacy with the Father that we will begin seeing what He is doing, and He will begin sharing the secrets of His heart with us. The Holy Spirit and the angels are waiting for sons and daughters of God to open their mouths and speak.

As you develop your relationship with Him, He will teach you how to co labour with Him. I believe Charles Frances used to teach that the operating of working of miracles, was when God showed you something specific to do to co-labour with Christ to manifest a miracle in someone's body. This definition of the gifting makes so much sense to me, and I believe this is how Jesus operated – the Father would show Jesus what to do or say to make a miracle or healing manifest, and we should operate in the same way. If you look at the life of Jesus He never really healed the sick the same way twice, He was always doing something different.

There are many different ways that God has used me to heal the sick in the last few years, however none of these can be limited to a method because each miracle occurred because I saw or heard what the Father was doing, and I obeyed. Obedience, when operating with the Holy Spirit to perform miracles, is crucial. We must be led by Him, and obey. Many of the nine gifts operate together a lot of the time, especially the gift of healing, working of miracles, faith and words of knowledge. These gifts are released through the Holy Spirit and a lot of the time are also enforced through angelic beings. I'll share some examples of how I have seen people healed over the last few years, operating in these gifts and with angels, and will explain in a little more detail the gifts.

We went to a hospital in Nantes, France to pray for a man who wasn't a Christian, and was in really bad shape. He was depressed and his head was in pain because he had an abyss on his brain which caused swelling. He was weak, as he was throwing up a lot and couldn't drink water; he also had AIDS and cerebral meningitis. Just as we began to pray I saw a flash of light and knew an angel had entered the room. We began praying, and when we had finished Janet and Anne-Marie both saw a light shining on his head. We asked how he was and he said he had fire on his head and the pain was draining away, there was just a little bit left. His entire countenance changed; he was happy and thanking Jesus for His presence. He wasn't a Christian but he was saying, "thank you Jesus." He was encountering God in the bed and we began prophesying his character to him, and he confirmed we were right. Then we said, "God showed us this because He loves you." and he said, "I knew about God but I never knew He loved me until today." He had an encounter with the love of Jesus and he was so thankful that we came. A couple of days later he left the hospital completely well after what he called his Jesus party. When I recognised the angelic was ministering with me, it boosted my faith that the miracle was about to take place. We need to learn to recognise and cooperate with the angelic beings around our lives.

I was in Mexico and we were running a small meeting of around twenty women in a person's house. Every one of the women was totally healed. One lady came forward and was 80% blind due to cataracts. While I was praying for her I saw angels with windscreen wipers wiping the cataracts out of her eyes, and so I copied what they were doing; she opened her eyes and burst into tears totally healed. We need to see what is happening in the invisible realm and manifest it in the natural.

In the same meeting, I was standing in front of a window and saw the sun come up behind me and my shadow appeared in the room. I remembered the story of Peter's shadow healing the sick, and I felt like the Holy Spirit said He wanted to do the same thing again. So I asked the next person to stand in my shadow,

I can't completely remember the person's condition however I believe it was bad back pain. They stood in my shadow and without even praying they were instantly healed. I had my interpreter stand there next, and three times in a row people were healed standing in our shadows. These past two testimonies were operating in the gift of 'working of miracle's and 'gift of faith' I believe these two gifts most often work hand in hand, the Father showed us something to do to co-labour with him to manifest the miracles, and by faith, we obeyed.

People have even been getting healed by accident. I was standing, before a meeting, greeting people in England and I was talking to a lady for a few minutes. After around 5 minutes she said, "as soon as you walked up to me my shoulder and leg began getting really hot." I asked her if she had problems or pain in those areas and she said she did. I asked her to begin moving and seeing how the pain was, she moved and realised she was totally healed, just being in the presence of God. I had no idea she had any problems.

Recently in Sydney, I was going down a ministry line and a lady just walked away before I got to her. Later I found out she had torn ligaments in her shoulder and was in lots of pain, and couldn't raise her arm, but as she was standing in line she realised she was completely healed and didn't require prayer so she left the line.

Also in Sydney, a lady had a sore heel causing her to limp, I got there and the Holy Spirit said get her to hop twice on her foot and test it. I told her, and she hopped and was instantly healed, to her surprise.

I was on the Sunshine Coast and during worship I saw a picture (vision) of a 13 year old boy with asthma who I took up the front, had people run around him in a circle, and he was healed. So when it came time for me to do ministry, I called out if anyone had asthma, one kid raised his hand and I pointed and asked if he was 13 and he said yes, so I told the church the rest of my vision. He came forward with 2 others who had asthma. I gathered some youth and had all of us run around them in a circle 4 times, sent them outside, and all 3 were completely healed. I saw the boy a few weeks later and he was still totally fine. This is a great example of the gift of 'word of knowledge' and 'operating of miracles' working together.

A word of knowledge is simply a fact or piece of information from the Holy Spirit that you can't possibly know without Him, that you can test right now. In my example above, the word of knowledge was that there was a 13 year old boy with Asthma, which is a testable fact. The operating in miracles was God showing me to get him out the front and have the people run around him to manifest the miracle.

I was in Mexico at a women's meeting and the presence of God was so thick I really felt like I didn't need to do anything, so as I was on stage I began calling out words of knowledge, then I had people stand up, and around 30-40 people stood. I felt like we didn't even need to pray and told them to begin testing their bodies to see what God was doing. People started moving and one lady waved at me, I asked her to shout out what was happening and she released her testimony to the crowd. Then I told them that her testimony had released more power in the room for the rest of them to be healed. One by one I watched in amazement as every single woman standing was completely healed without us even having to pray for one of them. This is a great example of the power of words of knowledge; when a word is released it carries the power within it to release the healing. Words of knowledge also increase faith in the people who receive the word, often times it will be when people respond to the word and apply their faith to receive, that they will be healed.

I was in Mexico in a house with 4 people and I was about to pray for a lady with arthritis in her knees and elbows, I grabbed her hands and was about to pray when I heard the Holy Spirit say, "don't pray." Then I saw a clock with a count down on it in my head, I watched and when it reached zero I let go and asked her to test it out. I could see the look on her face saying but you haven't done anything yet, but she began moving around and then burst into tears realising that all the pain was gone from her joints. She ran up and down the stairs completely healed.

I was in South Africa in a house meeting and one of the guys had a bad migraine, 7 out of 10 pain level. He had been thinking about not coming to the meeting but came anyway. We got a word of knowledge and I went to pray. I heard the Holy Spirit say put him in an elevator, so I asked him to close his eyes and pretend he was in an elevator, he was on level 7 and I asked him to press the number that he wanted the pain to be at, so he reached out and pressed 0. Then I did some music for him and told him to tell me when he got to the ground floor, he said he was there and I asked him how he was feeling, to his surprise all the pain in his head was gone.

The first miracle I was ever involved with was a woman sitting next to me in a meeting, she had a frozen shoulder and couldn't raise her arm. I prayed for her and she felt fire go through her shoulder, then she started raising her arm, but it still wouldn't move. I felt like I should grab her arm and raise it above her head, so I grabbed her arm and slowly began raising it. You could see she was surprised and was waiting for the pain to kick in, but it never did, and her arm was above her head when she realised she was healed. In this instance I'm not sure what came over me to raise her arm above her head, and I believe the gift of 'faith' was operating in this circumstance.

All of these testimonies are simply to show you that healing is really easy when you make it about Jesus. You just need to be in relationship with Him and stay in tune with what He is doing and saying, then be absolutely obedient when you hear Him say something. If you do it without hesitating, this will release an increase in the miraculous in your life. There is no formula, each time could be completely different, this is how Jesus ministry looked when He was walking the earth.

However, do you realise that operating in working of miracles, gifts of healings, faith and words of knowledge all require you to take a step of faith? John Wimber spelt faith *risk*, the only way you will ever operate in healing, miracles, or any power, is to live a lifestyle of *risk*. You see the only way you learn to distinguish if it is the voice of Jesus that is telling you to do these things or not, is to actually try. It is when you take that risk that you learn whether it is something you made up or whether it was the voice of God. If it doesn't work then apologise because it wasn't what God was saying, if it was it would have worked. As churches, we need to begin creating a culture of celebrating risk rather than what the world perceives as success. We need to redefine what success looks like. I had to personally change this definition in my own life. I used to think I was a failure if I went to the streets and asked to pray for people and they weren't healed, or saved or I was rejected. However, I changed my definition of success, now if I approach someone and they feel loved, they have experienced an encounter with the love of God, and I am successful.

My only job is to love every person who is placed in front of me, or every person I encounter. It is impossible to fail if we approach people out of love. What are all the testimonies that we hear in church? I asked a person if I could pray for them and they got radically healed and saved. How many people do you hear coming to church saying, "I approached a person this week and asked if I could pray for them, and they said 'no way get lost,' so I told them Jesus loves them and blessed them on their way." We should be celebrating that testimony just as loudly as the first one.

Operating in Healing and Miracles

God showed me a picture one time of when I prayed for someone. Do you know what I found out? The time when Jesus got a huge smile on His face, and started celebrating, wasn't at the very end when He found out the result of my encounter. His celebrating started the second I decided to step over the chicken line and take a risk. You see we can't determine the results of whether someone gets healed or not, it is our job to step out in faith and love the person. Faith is what pleases God, and it is the act of taking that initial step of faith, to decide to encounter someone, that brings so much pleasure to Jesus. We should be celebrating like Jesus, we need to be encouraging people and celebrating when they take risk, not just when they see results.

Many people ask me, "what do you focus on when you pray?" Personally, I focus on Jesus; how big and good He is, I remember His compassion for the person in front of me and that He wants them healed more than I do. I remember that I am one with Him, and that the fullness of the Holy Spirit lives in me. I see Him in me, flowing through my body into the person to whom I am ministering. Many times I also enter the Spirit and take the spirit of the person to whom I am ministering before Jesus in the throne room. No matter what their condition is they are totally whole in heaven, then I pray from that place of seeing them whole and release the power for it to manifest on earth. You see, on earth you see the problem, but when you take them to heaven all you can see is the solution. When you begin to look through the eyes of Jesus you will be consumed with the answer and will see them whole. Then you speak that reality into being on the earth.

Now I want to make something very clear as well, healing is not dependent on seeing, hearing or feeling, these are just tools or ways that God helps us to co-labour with Him. The majority of the time I actually feel nothing when I pray for the sick, however I am beginning to feel more often. Most of the time I simply lay my hands on a sick person, I command them to be made well, and I believe that God will do His part because His word says lay hands on the sick and they shall recover in Mark 16.

The power of the Testimony

We need to feed on testimonies and we need to be good stewards of them. If you haven't seen anyone healed yet, then begin watching YouTube videos and listening to people share their testimonies, then take these as your own and begin sharing these testimonies with people. I watched hundreds of hours of YouTube videos of Todd White, A. A. Allen, William Branham, Oral Roberts and T.B. Joshua, to name a few, and then shared these testimonies with people as often as I could.

I read books full of testimonies and recite them to friends. I constantly have my mind focused on what God has done in the past, and what He will do in the future. You need to understand the power that is held within a testimony. Revelation 19:10 says "the testimony of Jesus is the spirit of prophecy."

Testimony in the Greek means *to do it again*, so when you share a testimony you are actually asking God to do it again. When you share a testimony, it releases the exact same power to be present to perform the same miracle again. Therefore, when I am ministering to someone, I almost always share a testimony of the same condition that the person I'm ministering to has, being healed. If I don't have one, I share another testimony, because testimonies also increase faith. This does not need to be a testimony that you have actually seen take place, because it does not say the testimony of (insert your name) is the spirit of prophecy. It says the testimony of Jesus and they are all His. I have given you dozens of testimonies throughout this material for you to begin sharing with people, and reading over. There are also many testimonies in the Bible, which are the best ones to read.

Practical tips to Ministering in Healing

What you give thanks for, increases. Jesus gave thanks for the fish and the bread and it multiplied, this is a biblical principle. As we pray for the sick, we need to make sure that we maintain our focus on what God is doing in a person's body, not on what isn't happening. We need to help a person to connect with the reality that Jesus is amongst them, and is touching them, because very often people are so focused on their problem that they can't see anything else. This leads us into the first tip when ministering to people.

Never allow people to pull you into their atmosphere of sympathy, because sympathy will lock a person in their problem, but compassion will pull them out. People love to talk about how badly they are doing and give you their entire life history. By the time they are finished you are left in a place with your eyes solely on their problem and how big it is, and have zero faith to now heal them. So as politely as you can sometimes, you need to interrupt people and say, "well let's just see what Jesus wants to do right now." Just get the information that you need to pray and then begin, you need to remain in a place with your eyes fixed on Jesus.

Recently I prayed for a girl who had a messed up back, slipped discs and constant pain, however, she also had a problem with excessive sweating in her hands. I prayed for her back and when she bent over, and all the pain disappeared, she'd had this problem for 9 years so you would think she might be excited. All she said was, "but my hands aren't healed." I said, "yeah but your back is healed." and she said, "but my hands." I said, "let's pause for a moment, I'm going to pray for your hands but let's thank Jesus for what He has done in your back, because I couldn't have taken the pain away, which means that Jesus is here with us and He is healing you." We gave thanks then I prayed for her hands and the sweat disappeared under my hands.

We need to always take peoples' attention and focus them on what God is doing. I pray for someone and then I ask them "what's different?" We need to expect that something has changed when we pray for them. It is impossible to pray and have nothing happen. Then focus on whatever they tell you, if the pain is still there but they felt a slight tingle on their big toe, then begin thanking God for the tingle of His presence and pray again. If nothing happens don't be discouraged, just pray again and test.

I prayed for a man in Nebraska one time who had badly damaged his Achilles tendon and was in 10 out of 10 pain. I prayed for him and asked him to test it, nothing, prayed again, nothing happened. I prayed 12 times and there was no change in his ankle. Who knows that if I had given up at this point or any previous point this man may not have received his miracle? However, I had a silent prayer with God and said, "Papa just let me see some change in this next prayer and I'll know he will be healed." I prayed again, for the thirteenth time, and he said, "well the pain is now at 9.5." I got super excited and started thanking God and celebrating for the 0.5 decrease because I knew we had it. I didn't need to pray again, the man came back three days later and told me that as soon as he had walked out of the building that night, all the pain disappeared from his ankle and he was healed. Continually give thanks each time for whatever is different even if the pain drop seems as insignificant as 0.5. I always tell people, well I can't make your pain decrease 0.5 percent so that must mean God is here and He is healing you. Help the person to connect with the presence of God; this will make them better receivers for the next round. Often, we have seen people healed simply by saying 'thanks Jesus,' and testing again. Often times a person's breakthrough might be just the other side of convenience. What if I had stopped praying after prayer number 5? Sometimes a person's miracle manifests as they begin testing.

One of the most important keys I can give you, when ministering in healing, is always to have the person test and try to do something that they couldn't do before. Jesus would always give a person something to do to activate their faith, and cooperate in the miracle. In Matthew 12:13 "Then he said to the man, "Stretch out your hand." So he stretched it out and it was completely restored, just as sound as the other." In John 5:8-9 "Jesus said to him, "Get up! Pick up your mat and walk." At once the man was cured; he picked up his mat and walked." John 9:7 "Go," he told him, "wash in the Pool of Siloam". So the man went and washed, and came home seeing."

These are just a couple of examples, there are many more. He told the lepers to show themselves to the priest: each time He would give people something to do. We need to do the same, ask the person to do something they couldn't do before. This requires wisdom, if someone has a broken foot don't ask them to jump up and down on it, you can ask them to try moving their toes slightly. You don't need to ask them to do a monumental act of faith, just try something small and simple.

I prayed for a man with a destroyed knee and he had a whole leg brace on.

I prayed and asked him to put some weight on his foot to see if the pain had decreased. He realised there was no more pain and then I asked if we could take the brace off, which we did, and he was healed. Just something small is fine, God is simply looking for a step of faith no matter how small. In the past I used to pray for people, bless them and leave. I wouldn't ask them to test it because I didn't truly believe that anything was going to happen instantly. However, faith believes that when I lay my hands on the sick they will be healed. I have seen a dramatic increase in miracles as I have started to pray less and ask them to test more.

You see we don't need to pray 15 minute prayers to heal the sick. Many times in the past I was praying long prayers, because I didn't really think anything was going to happen, and I was scared to stop and have to test it out. Other times I wanted to make sure that the person knew I was taking this seriously, so I would put on a show with my best prayer. However, who knows that Jesus didn't pray long prayers? If you want a successful healing ministry, do what Jesus did, He used just a few words most of the time. Look at the previous passages I mentioned, His longest prayer was 8 words. He cast out demons with a word in Matthew 8. He doesn't take a long time to heal people and He isn't deaf, we don't need to beg, instead we declare. Jesus didn't tell us to pray for the sick He commanded us to *heal* the sick.

My mentor Chris Gore would often say "Do you know that your prayers don't heal the sick? If that was the case I could write a book of prayers guaranteed to heal the sick and become a millionaire overnight." It is not your prayers that heal the sick, it is Jesus who heals the sick, it is Him in and through you.

Operating out of Rest

Everything in the kingdom is conducted from a place of rest. We need to learn to work from the rest of God, and we will begin to accomplish much more for the kingdom. God showed me, a few times, pictures of eagles soaring high above the clouds. Eagles are a unique creature. Most birds use a lot of energy and have to flap constantly to get as high as eagles can fly. Eagles, however, simply flap a few times and then rest and position themselves in the air currents, to allow them to go higher than the other birds, and stop them from being worn out. They can do a lot of work with minimal energy expenditure, because they position themselves in the correct place.

The Holy Spirit showed me that we are like the eagles, and if we position ourselves in the air current of God's love, and the presence of the Holy Spirit, He will do the work for us and take us places that our effort could never get us. We will accomplish more by spending time in the presence of God than we could ever do in our own strength. Healing the sick is all about resting in the finished work of the cross, understanding that Jesus already paid the price. So, through relationship with Him and yielding to the Holy Spirit, He will flow through us to touch the sick and heal them. Resting in our identity and authority as sons, we don't need to fight for a victory because Jesus won the victory. We get to fight from His victory. As we rest and receive how much God loves us, the supernatural will flow naturally from us. Both the fruit and the gifts of the spirit will operate through us as we pursue love.

Your Turn

I hope that as I have shared my story and the testimonies of what God has done in and through my life, that you have been both challenged and inspired. Don't let this be another book that you simply read and gather more information. I have given you many practical activations and exercises to deepen your relationship with the Lord. Do these activations and begin pursuing an even greater depth of relationship with God; He is waiting and longing to know you in a deeper way. Through this book, you have learnt that you are a son or a daughter, totally loved by the Father, the righteousness of God. You have access to an intimate relationship with the Lord. You have learnt a number of different tools to build your secret place with the Lord, and take your relationship to the next level. You've learnt about, worship, humility and surrender.

I pray that the eyes of your heart have been enlightened in the knowledge of Him. I pray every blessing upon your life, and an impartation, from the reading of this book, for revelation of your identity, a fresh longing to know Christ, and an increase in anointing to walk in the power of God and advance the Kingdom with signs and wonders.

You have now joined the army of the Lord. Spread the word that the kingdom of heaven is at hand, heal the sick, cast out demons and raise the dead! The next step is yours.

Will you begin the journey of Cultivating a Life of Power?

About the Author

Jason and Melissa Rawlings are the founders of Roar and Soar Ministries.

Their mission is to train an army of warriors in identity, intimacy and power.

Jason has taught in many different churches and countries with a passion to equip the body of Christ. There are many miracles, signs and wonders witnessed in his meetings. He lives with his wife Melissa on the Gold Coast in Australia.

To contact Roar and Soar Ministries visit
www.roarandsoarministries.com.au
or email
roarandsoarministries@gmail.com

To invite Jason Rawlings to speak at your ministry please complete the form at
www.roarandsoarministries.com.au/invite-jason-to-speak/

www.ingramcontent.com/pod-product-compliance
Lightning Source LLC
Chambersburg PA
CBHW051948290426
44110CB00015B/2160